Knowing the Spirit

Knowing the Spirit

OSTAD ELAHI

Translated and with an Introduction by
James Winston Morris

STATE UNIVERSITY OF NEW YORK PRESS

Cover photo of Ostad Elahi used by kind permission of Fondation Ostad Elahi

Published by
State University of New York Press, Albany

© 2007 State University of New York

For information, address State University of New York Press,
194 Washington Avenue, Suite 305, Albany, NY 12210-2384

Production by Kelli Williams
Marketing by Fran Keneston

Library of Congress Cataloging-in-Publication Data

Ilahi, Nur 'Ali, 1897–
  [Ma'rifat al-ruh. English]
  Knowing the spirit / Ostad Elahi ; translated and with an introduction by James
Winston Morris.
      p. cm.
  Includes bibliographical references and index.
  ISBN-13: 978-0-7914-6857-9 (hardcover : alk. paper)
  ISBN-10: 0-7914-6857-7 (hardcover : alk. paper)
  ISBN-13: 978-0-7914-6858-6 (pbk. : alk. paper)
  ISBN-10: 0-7914-6858-5 (pbk. : alk. paper)
  1. Soul—Islam. I. Morris, James Winston, 1949– II. Title.

BP166.73.I413 2006
297.2'25—dc22   2005036232

10 9 8 7 6 5 4 3 2 1

Contents

Preface and Acknowledgements

Knowing the Spirit, like the rest of Ostad Elahi's writings and teaching, is intended as a kind of bridge: a bridge meant to be open and accessible to each reader, but in ways necessarily reflecting their own particular experience and understanding. One could describe this type of writing in the same terms that the author himself uses here to describe each soul's actual experience of the spiritual world: "it is like a mirror: everyone sees their own form in it." The introduction and notes accompanying this translation are designed to help restore that original directness of expression and accessibility for today's readers in English, who necessarily approach this book from a very different cultural background.

Historically, *Knowing the Spirit* can be seen as a bridge between the intellect and spiritual experience (*'aql* and *kashf*), between the learned philosophical and metaphysical traditions of Iran and the complex forms of spiritual practice, contemplation, and guidance traditionally associated with Sufism and the wider expressions of Islamic spirituality.

At the same time, given worldwide transformations in the actual conditions of religious and spiritual life, changes that were especially dramatic during Ostad Elahi's own lifetime (1895–1974), this book also provides us with a remarkable bridge between the world's major religions, in that it constantly points to the fundamental, shared human realities and dimensions of experience underlying the often puzzling symbolic presentations of eschatology and metaphysical teaching within each of those traditions. As such, like the rest of Ostad Elahi's teaching, it suggests a way leading toward the gradual emergence of what has recently been called the nascent "science of spirituality."

Finally, and most intimately, the author's guiding metaphysical vision of human destiny, of the true universality of the processes of spiritual realization, offers a helpful bridge toward the actual ongoing tasks of spiritual intelligence, toward the unfolding interplay of experience and understanding within each reader's own path of spiritual perfection.

Special thanks are due first of all to those many friends, colleagues and former students who have patiently read through and helped clarify earlier drafts of this translation and introduction, including most recently my editor at State University of New York Press, Nancy Ellegate. At the same time, the essential understanding and presentation of this volume were based on years of study of related traditions of Islamic thought and spirituality, especially the writings of Ibn 'Arabi, Mulla Sadra, and the great Persian mystical poets. Since it would take many pages to list all the scholars and colleagues who have aided those supporting studies, I can only acknowledge here by name those first, now-departed teachers who so memorably started me on that long path: S. J. Ashtiyani, Henry Corbin, Toshihiko Izutzu, and Annemarie Schimmel.

The final completion of this project was greatly facilitated by a study leave from the University of Exeter, and I am particularly grateful to the Fondation Ostad Elahi (together with its President, Dr. Bahram Elahi) for granting the translation rights for *Ma'rifat ar-Rūh*. As with all of my work, this book would not have reached completion without the editorial vigilance, encouragement, and constant support of my wife Corey.

—James Winston Morris

Translator's Introduction

The subject of *Ma'rifat ar-Rūh* (*Knowing the Spirit*)—the divine Spirit (*rūh*) and the process of spiritual perfection of the human soul (also one of the key meanings of *rūh* here)[1]—is of intimate interest to every human being. And what Ostad Elahi, its author, has to say here about that subject has rarely been presented in such clear and explicit terms. However, the technical language and formal style he used in this work reflected the complex traditions of later Islamic philosophy, spirituality, and theology familiar to his original audience of traditionally educated scholars, so that today many of his assumptions and allusions tailored to that traditionally bilingual (Persian and Arabic) scholarly audience are difficult to follow even for contemporary readers fluent in Persian. This introduction is intended to provide the considerable amount of essential contextual and background information most readers today will need to appreciate the author's universal intentions and meanings, beginning with (I) a brief overview of his life and works, moving on to outline (II) those particular assumptions and expectations of his original learned audience that need further explanation for today's readers. A final section (III) then briefly highlights some of those more original developments in spirituality, psychology, and spiritual ethics that help account for the ongoing contemporary relevance of this work, especially in the fields of comparative spirituality and philosophy, psychology, and the study of religion.

Readers who wish to move on immediately to discovering Ostad Elahi's key ideas, in his own words, should note that he has greatly facilitated their task by carefully underlining in each chapter those few short phrases (given in ***italic boldface*** in this translation) where he explicitly summarized the essence of his own personal understanding of this immense subject.[2] Most of those summary passages are in the form of highly condensed allusions that are clearly meant to be the subject of extended meditation and reflection, to be verified and illustrated above all in light of the reader's own experiences and spiritual

1

intelligence. Throughout this book, which the author repeatedly tells us he intentionally composed at a condensed and highly abstract level of metaphysical concision, he carefully leaves it to each reader to supply the indispensable (and necessarily highly personal) probative experiences and "spiritual phenomenology" that alone can translate these philosophical and theological concepts and symbols into actual *knowing*.

That guiding intention is explicitly signaled in the opening word of Ostad Elahi's title: *ma'rifa* is the technical term traditionally used in Islamic spirituality to specify the necessarily individual, active awareness that is the accomplished fruit of direct, personal spiritual experience and contemplation: that is, the *realized* state of actual spiritual insight and understanding, not the more abstract, conceptual forms of "knowledge."[3] Ostad Elahi's intention here, as he makes clear from the very start, is to awaken each reader's inner awareness and deeper understanding of that which constitutes what we really are. Reminding us of that, his first highlighted passage, at the very beginning of this book, stresses that it was composed as an answer to "the requests of those who are following a path of spiritual guidance."

I. Ostad Elahi's Life and Works

Nūr 'Alī Elāhī—or Ostad Elahi ("Master" Elahi), the honorific by which he is most widely known today—was born on September 11, 1895 in Jeyhunabad, a village in western Iran.[4] The outward course of his life, as he described it in autobiographical conversations and remarks during his later years,[5] falls into three distinct periods: his childhood and youth, entirely devoted to traditional forms of ascetic and religious training; his active public career, for almost thirty years, as a prosecutor, magistrate, and high-ranking judge; and the period of his retirement, more openly devoted to spiritual teaching and writing (including the composition of *Knowing the Spirit*), when he became well known as a religious thinker, philosopher, and theologian, as well as a musician. Ostad Elahi's own later description of those outward events, summarized in a few of his sayings quoted further on, helps bring out the inner connections between those different periods of his life and the broader lessons he was able to draw from those very different activities and experiences.

Childhood and Youth

Ostad Elahi's father, Hajj Ni'mat Jayhunabadi (1873–1920), was a prolific writer and mystical poet, from a locally prominent family.[6] Among his many writings was his major work *The Book of Kings of the Truth*,[7] an immense poetic compendium of traditional spiritual teachings. From early childhood on, Ostad Elahi led an ascetic, secluded life of rigorous spiritual discipline under his father's watchful supervision. He also received the general classical education of that time, with its special focus on religious and ethical instruction as the foundation of his training. It was during those formative years of his youth, completely devoted to contemplation and study, that he developed the basic foundations of his later philosophic and spiritual thinking. In his own words:

> I began fasting and spiritual exercises at the age of nine, and kept them up continuously for almost twelve years, taking only a few days between the forty-day periods of spiritual retreat. Usually my evening meal to break the fast was only bread and vinegar. I almost never went out of the retreat house, and I only associated with the seven or eight dervishes who were allowed to enter it. When I finally left the retreat house at the end of those twelve years and came into contact with other people, I couldn't imagine that it was even possible for human beings to tell lies.[8]

The following story poignantly conveys both the special role of his father's guidance in that initial stage of his spiritual discipline and the lasting lessons that he was able to draw from that intense period of spiritual training:

> Ordinarily during my childhood I was always involved in spiritual exercises. Only occasionally did we have a few days' break between two forty-day periods of spiritual retreat and fasting. During one of those periods of spiritual retreat, someone brought me two strings of delicious dried figs. I set them aside specially for myself, and each night I broke my fast in a state of intense desire for those figs; after breaking the fast I would take great pleasure in eating a few of them, until the forty days were over. On the last night of the retreat I had a dream in which I saw each person's spiritual exercises being recorded. I saw my own as a wall that I had built with beautiful bricks, except that a corner of each brick was broken off and incomplete. . . . The next day my mother, as she usually did, asked my father's permission to prepare an offering meal. "No," my father

replied, "because this person's spiritual exercise is imperfect, he'll have to perform another forty days of fasting and
retreat, as a fine, so that his mind won't be filled with figs."
The point of this is that the essential condition for spiritual
exercise and fasting is not just doing without food. Rather,
the person traveling the spiritual path must always have
their attention on the Source and must cut their attachments to everything else. Otherwise, there are plenty of
people who go without eating something. (AH, 1877)

Ostad Elahi's lifelong devotion to spiritual music, and in particular his mastery of the *tanbūr* (a lutelike stringed instrument especially
used for gatherings of religious music and prayer), also date from his
early childhood: "There are two things to which I've always unspar-
ingly given my time: one is the *tanbūr* and the other is traveling the
spiritual Path."[9] The following story illustrates not only the role of
music already in Ostad Elahi's childhood, but also the special inner
affinity with nature and other creatures which was a distinctive trait
of his character throughout his life:

When I was a child, they brought me a partridge one day.
That partridge loved the sound of the *tanbūr*. As soon as I
picked up my instrument, the bird would sit right next to
me. And once I started playing she would become intoxi-
cated by the music and begin to sing, gripping my hand and
pecking at it with her beak; that state of drunkenness made
her completely wild. At night, the partridge slept on a shelf
in my room. Early one morning, when I wanted to go back
to sleep, she began to sing. I grumbled at her to be quiet; and
immediately she lowered her head sadly and stopped sing-
ing. From that day on, whenever the partridge woke up in
the early morning, she would stand at the foot of my bed
and pull softly on the covers, cooing softly. If I didn't react,
after two or three tries she understood that I was still sleeping and went away. But if I said to her "Mmmh, what a
pretty voice!" she would begin to sing. (AH, vol. 2, 162)

While the outward course of Ostad Elahi's life was eventually to
take him away from this purely contemplative, traditional way of life,
he always continued to acknowledge the foundational role of this early
period of spiritual discipline and retreat and his father's guidance
during that time:

My mother was anxious about my worldly education, and she always used to ask my father: "So when is he going to do his studies?" My father replied: "As long as his domineering self (*nafs*) hasn't awakened, let him complete his spiritual training, so that it won't be able to have an effect on him. After that he'll study." Things turned out exactly as my father had predicted. I began my spiritual training when I was nine, and that course of spiritual discipline lasted for twelve years. After that I began to study, and desires and passions no longer had any effect on me. (AH, 1964)

Professional Life and Judicial Career

Some ten years after his father's death in 1920, Ostad Elahi left his spiritual retreat and eventually settled in Tehran, where he worked in the Registry Office and began to study civil law. This radical change of life was a sharp break with the local tradition, which would have destined him to an entirely contemplative way of life. This change of life, as he later explained, was necessary for him in order to deepen his thinking and to test his ethical and religious principles in the face of all the difficult demands of social and professional life.

God made me enter the public administration and government work despite my own aversion for that. He made me become a judge by force and gave me difficult judicial assignments. But afterwards I discovered that in each of those posts were concealed thousands of points of wisdom, such that even a multitude of philosophers and sages gathered together couldn't have designed such plans. (AH, 1966)

In 1933, Ostad Elahi successfully completed his studies at the national school for judicial officials. His professional abilities and sense of equity and good judgment were quickly recognized, so that he was invariably entrusted with responsibility for the most difficult assignments. A number of dramatic incidents came to demonstrate the truth of his later observation, "When I was a judge I was always prepared to be permanently dismissed rather than hand down a single judgment contrary to what was right and just" (AH, 2037). For almost thirty years he was appointed to positions of increasing responsibility throughout the country, sometimes as public prosecutor or examining magistrate, and eventually as an associate justice and then president of the Court of Appeals.

Throughout this period of his career as a magistrate, Ostad Elahi continued to devote a great deal of time to his personal studies and research, especially in the areas of philosophy and theology. Although we know little about the unfolding course of his thought during those years, it is clear that this period was extremely productive and filled with all sorts of experiences that richly nourished his studies and helped him to elaborate his later works. One of the stories he later recounted from that period vividly illustrates the broader spiritual lessons he drew from the experiences of that time:

> During the time I was an investigative magistrate in Shiraz, I hadn't brought my family along with me. I rented part of a house; the owner occupied one side of the house, and I lived on the other side. One night a special spiritual state came over me, and I wanted to pass the night in solitude and seclusion, concentrating on prayer and meditation and my own spiritual state. The owner of the house had invited lots of people, and it was getting noisy. . . . I shut my door and opened my window facing the street, but there were two porters just outside beneath the window, who were busy discussing their problems. So I closed the window and went up on the roof, but there were already two women up there talking. I had to climb down, and I went off to visit a local saint's shrine. The guardian of that shrine was an upright and respected dervish. "I'm going into your room and I want to concentrate on my spiritual state," I told him. "Please don't let anyone come in and disturb my retreat." He agreed, so I went on into his room, still wanting to devote myself to that spiritual state. Just at that moment two women came up and began to joke around with that guardian, who was more than a hundred years old. I was at the end of my rope. I came out of the room and asked them to leave the dervish alone, but it turned out they wanted to chat with me too! In short, that special state of mine disappeared; and no matter what I did I wasn't able to concentrate. "O Lord," I said, "so you're still testing me? Well by God, it's up to You. Thy will be done!"

> Later on, in the spiritual world, they told me that the aim of all this was to prevent me from secluding myself, because I'd recently been a little too withdrawn, and that I

ought to participate in social occasions in accordance with my profession. It's not right to try to withdraw from society. Instead you must go out into society while still staying true to your self. . . . To be in society and still remain moral, that's what counts. (AH, 1924)

Throughout this period, spiritual music continued to have a very important place in Ostad Elahi's life. He was soon acknowledged by musical specialists to be a great virtuoso of the *tanbūr*, and he enriched its repertoire by composing many original musical pieces of his own. This musical practice and creation was always integrally connected with his wider spiritual life, as one can see in such remarks as the following: "I'm always thinking of my master. In music, whenever I play a piece or a melody I've learned from someone, I say a prayer for that person if they're still alive; and if they're dead, I ask God's mercy for them" (AH, 1950).

In his lessons and oral teachings given later in life, Ostad Elahi often illustrated his points with anecdotes drawn from this period, in a way that suggests how he was able to discover profound spiritual lessons in the "ordinary" encounters and incidents each day brings. As he once put it, "It is in everyday life that I've learned the most lessons about the underlying order of the universe. This world becomes a place for spiritual edification once we discover how to draw those lessons from it—even from the flight of a mosquito." The following memorable story is a typical example:

One day, during the time I was head of the court in Jahrom, I was outside of town when I saw a very beautiful orchard and fields out in the middle of the desert. I asked whose it was, and they told me: "It belongs to a person who started out with absolutely nothing and has now come to this point. One day he was passing by there when he noticed some moisture under the rocks on the surface. He dug down a little deeper with his walking stick and saw that the wetness increased. With a great deal of toil and trouble he constructed an irrigation tunnel, and now he's been busy with that for some twenty years." Later I met that man, and I was very friendly and encouraging with him. As he described himself: "When I first came here I was alone and without any money. I had just enough to buy a bucket and a shovel, but with a lot of hard work I was able to channel the water, and now I've reached this point." All those orchards and fields he had were the result of this principle of persistence and perseverance. (AH, 1936)

Another similar personal story, from somewhat later in his life, also illustrates the sense of humor that was always one of his distinctive traits of character:

Last night I woke up at midnight as usual for my nightly prayers and devotions. But because I was feeling slightly ill I acted a bit lazy and said to myself: "I'll pray tomorrow morning," and I went back to sleep. Of course the next morning I performed my prayers, and then I began to do my exercises. Now I had never dropped one of the exercise weights before, but one of those weights slipped out of my hand and fell right on my toes. It hurt for an hour. God had reprimanded me to exactly the same extent as I'd been lazy with Him—there was something almost comical about it! I was extremely happy about that incident, and I bowed down to God in gratitude on the spot. "Now I know that You love me," I told him, "and that You're always watching over me. Otherwise I might have been lazy other nights as well." (AH, 2002)

One final incident dating from this period strikingly underlines yet another key aspect of Ostad Elahi's character that is evident in all of his teaching, which was his own rigorous insistence on actually *living*, practicing and clearly demonstrating through one's own life and actions the abstract principles of spiritual and religious truth. A student of his noted that one day while Ostad Elahi was explaining that we should not reject other religions and faiths, he added by way of illustration:

One time in Kermanshah, while I was out walking with a group of friends, we passed by a place where some Jews were praying. To the bewilderment of my companions, I went in and began to pray along with them. At first those in the synagogue thought I was trying to make fun of them; but when they understood that that wasn't the case, they were very pleased. We should never miss an occasion to pray under the pretext that it would involve praying with Jews, Christians, Muslims, or any others. (AH, vol. 2, 43)

The Final Period: Writing and Teaching

Ostad Elahi retired from the judiciary in 1957, and only after that did he really begin to discuss more publicly his own way of thinking. During this period he published two major scholarly works, *Knowing the Spirit* (*Ma'rifat ar-Rūh*) and *Burhān al-Haqq* (*Demonstration of the Truth*), which were authoritative statements in their respective fields, as well as an extensive commentary on his father's immense spiritual epic.[10] At the same time, he began to develop much more fully the practical spiritual dimension of his teaching through the oral teachings and instruction that he shared with a few friends and students who gathered with him at his home until the end of his life, in 1974. Two lengthy volumes of Ostad Elahi's sayings and spiritual teachings—including all the anecdotes cited previously—have so far been published on the basis of notes written down by his students during that period.[11]

Those collected sayings bear the marks of profound spiritual inspiration, while they also reveal a penetrating understanding of human nature, a constant concern for intelligibility, and the sensitive use of immense learning in the service of a creative and original way of thinking. The following concluding remarks, from the last years of Ostad Elahi's life, beautifully highlight the source and intentions of his later spiritual teaching and the way all his instruction continued to be drawn from his own experience and practice:

> I have not passed over any subject in silence: all that is needed is a grasp of the question and the aspiration (to understand). And that aspiration comes from the angelic *spirit*. In these things I say to you my purpose is not to recount stories, but to give you sound advice. I am not able to tell someone something until after I've put it into practice and tried it out for myself. As for the points that I do mention, I won't express anything until I have completely investigated it to such a degree that no one could object to it, whether in this world or the next. I have spoken with each person to the extent that they could understand. But I've still not told anyone all there is in my heart. (AH, 2074)

> These are the things that I'll always love, that will please me and make my spirit rejoice even if I'm no longer in this world: to see those close to me wholeheartedly united and

working together, not squabbling and thinking of themselves; to see them striving to do what is good and to serve
others, always eager to act humanely, for the sake of others,
and truly to care for them. (AH, 2026)

Ostad Elahi's Published Works: The Place of Knowing the Spirit

Ostad Elahi continued to write on many subjects throughout his life,
as evidenced by the many unpublished notebooks and manuscripts
included in the exposition at the Sorbonne organized in celebration of
the centennial of his birth in 1995.[12] However, it was only after his
retirement from the judiciary that he began to publish his works,
beginning with the elaborate theological discussions of *Burhān al-Haqq*
(*Demonstration of the Truth*) in 1963, which was greatly expanded in
later editions; his commentary on his father's vast spiritual poem, the
Shāhnāmeh-ye Haqīqat, in 1966 (*Haqq al-Haqā'iq*); and finally the relatively much shorter volume of *Ma'rifat ar-Rūh* (*Knowing the Spirit*),
in 1969.

   Burhān al-Haqq is a highly complex theological and spiritual work,
dedicated to showing the inner concordance and common spiritual
aims shared by the Qur'an, the teachings of the Shiite Imams, and
original teachings and practices of the spiritual order of the "people of
the Truth" (*Ahl-i Haqq*), the dominant popular spiritual tradition in
Ostad Elahi's native region of western Iran, whose teachings and leg-
ends (originally transmitted in a rare regional Kurdish dialect) had
earlier been recorded in Persian verse in his father's immense *Book of
Kings of the Truth*.[13] Ostad Elahi's procedure in *Burhān al-Haqq* resembles
that of *Knowing the Spirit* insofar as he constantly juxtaposes the relevant scriptural verses of the Qur'an with the traditional Shiite teachings (and those of the great saints of the Ahl-i Haqq) in order to evoke
in his readers an awareness of the vast range of deeper shared spiritual truths underlying each of those traditions. The same metaphysical
issues central to *Knowing the Spirit* are often discussed there, but usually in more traditional symbolic and religious language; the explicitly
universal philosophical terminology and arguments adopted here are
not so much in evidence in that earlier volume.

   However, the essential bridge between *Burhān al-Haqq* and *Knowing the Spirit*—and in a way, to the more accessible and wide-ranging
oral spiritual discussions of that same period later revealed in detail
in *Athār al-Haqq*—was Ostad Elahi's constant concern with responding
to the spiritual questions and requests for guidance that he increasingly received from people in all walks of life, not only Iranians, but

now expanding to include famous scholars, musicians, students, and seekers who came to visit him from throughout Europe and America.[14] Thus the very genesis of *Knowing the Spirit*, as he points out in his introduction to this work, had to do with key questions first put to him about our knowledge and awareness of the "Spirit" by readers of *Burhān al-Haqq*. As a result of such questions, within a few years he began to add to his subsequent editions of *Burhān al-Haqq* (roughly two hundred pages in the original version) much longer appendixes" of more than four hundred additional pages, recording his responses to the very diverse spiritual questions of this multitude of inquiring visitors; many of those questions and responses extend far beyond the more limited, original theological contexts of that book.[15] As such, this first revealing summary of his actual personal efforts of teaching and guidance, in its later editions, was already almost as long as the more extensive verbatim collections of his oral teachings recorded in the later volumes of *Athār al-Haqq*.

II. Historical Contexts: The Audience, Language, and Structure of *Ma'rifat ar-Rūh*

As we have just pointed out, there is a marked contrast between the complex language and traditional forms of Ostad Elahi's published writings from the final period of his life (including *Knowing the Spirit*) and the simple, direct, highly anecdotal Persian of his oral teachings from that same time, collected and recorded in the volumes of *Athār al-Haqq*: for the most part, those oral teachings are quite readily understandable to readers today even in translation, with only minimal explanation of certain unfamiliar contexts and situations. Those two very different forms of written and oral expression were not due simply to different audiences and levels of education—since many of Ostad Elahi's interlocutors in the spiritual discussions recorded in *Athār al-Haqq* were themselves highly educated readers of *Knowing the Spirit* and other works like it—but rather to a complex set of long-standing cultural codes regarding the proper forms of educated *writing* (and likewise of *reading*), as distinguished from the more intimate realm of private oral discussion, which had been shared for centuries by writers and educated readers throughout the Islamic world. This section is intended to introduce as simply as possible some of those key traditional assumptions in ways that will help today's readers to better appreciate the meanings and intentions of *Knowing the Spirit*, beginning with some very general points and proceeding to more specific philosophical and theological background.

Indeed the most important assumption to keep in mind when reading this work can be stated very simply. Ostad Elahi implicitly expected his words to be read and reread slowly, reflectively, and repeatedly. And above all, he expected his ideal intended readers—who, he constantly reminds us, should be both "learned *and* spiritually insightful"—to provide their own indispensable reflections, applications, and experiential illustrations for each of the essential points summarized in his argument.[16] Only through such careful and actively participatory reading can his readers come to make the absolutely fundamental connections between the author's individual concepts and their own range of related spiritual experience, and thereby begin to perceive and explore the implications of each point and its essential interconnections with other observations developed elsewhere in this text. It is important to underline how radically this foundational assumption about the critical *active* role of the careful and properly qualified reader—once taken for granted by spiritual writers and readers in every civilization—contrasts with the basic rules and wider expectations of expository writing taken for granted in much of the world today: that is, with the familiar injunction to "keep it simple," begin with what is easiest for one's readers, identify carefully and explicitly each progressive stage of one's argument, always give memorable illustrations, and so on.

In the case of *Knowing the Spirit*, there is an especially clear connection between these basic wider assumptions of traditional esoteric writing and the particularly sensitive subject of Ostad Elahi's work: that is, the actual process of human spiritual perfection and destiny within its widest possible metaphysical context. That is because of two quite separate, but equally compelling, sets of considerations that still remain highly visible and problematic even today. First, for centuries, the official theological representatives of each of the Abrahamic religious traditions have usually carefully avoided serious *public* discussion of many of the most universal, phenomenological dimensions of spiritual life relating to the survival and gradual perfection of the human spirit—most obviously because such candidly descriptive spiritual discussions can so easily be seen as potentially undermining the central insistence, within each of those traditions, on the absolute importance of the responsible ethical actions and decisions of each moral actor here and now, within this immediate lifetime.[17] Needless to say, the actual situation in less public and politically sensitive contexts, especially within the disciplines of actual spiritual practice of each tradition, has always been far more complex and more accurately informed by the wider range of relevant spiritual experience. Second, whenever one approaches this problem (i.e., of the wider process of spiritual perfection) instead from the perspective of each *individual's* own limited set of relevant experiences and realizations, it is equally evident that all sorts of dangerous misunderstandings can immediately arise on the basis of each person's necessarily limited range of experience, partial views, common misinterpretations, the difficulty of fitting their individual experiences into larger perspectives of understanding (or belief), and so on. Almost all the distinctive features of Ostad Elahi's style of writing in *Knowing the Spirit* can be understood as a self-conscious, remarkably effective effort to deal with both of those twin dangers.

Finally, applying this basic principle of careful, actively participatory reading does partly presuppose some familiarity with the traditional fields of Islamic philosophy and theology (and related Arabic-language religious learning) that were central to the "general education" of the educated, literate classes in Iran during Ostad Elahi's youth—and indeed still are widely familiar in many circles, to a remarkable extent, down to our own day.[18] The following three sections introduce a few of the basic features of almost all writing within those traditions, which today's readers need to be aware of in order to appreciate the structure, aims, and distinctive rhetoric of *Knowing the Spirit*.

The "Three Sources": Rational Argument, Religious Tradition, and Spiritual Experience

One of the first things a reader must notice when first approaching *Knowing the Spirit* is the constant juxtaposition of philosophical arguments and reasoning; supporting passages from the Qur'an and reported sayings of earlier Islamic religious figures;[19] and—although this third aspect may be less obvious in the early chapters—allusions to the relevant range of actual human spiritual experience. At least since the time of the highly influential Iranian philosopher Mulla Sadra (d. 1640/1050),[20] it has been traditional for educated writers on all philosophical and related religious subjects, whether in Arabic or highly Arabicized Persian prose, to present their arguments and positions using supporting elements drawn from these same three foundational sources of rational argument (*'aql*), traditional religious sources (*naql*), and spiritual intuition (or "unveiling" and "direct personal witnessing": *kashf, shuhūd*). However, given the universality of this common scholastic literary tradition, it cannot be too strongly stressed that the recurrent references to these three different kinds of sources and discourse do not in any way represent a single outlook or approach. On the contrary, this agreed-upon language and style of presentation has normally been used for centuries to articulate and express every conceivable sort of philosophical and theological (and political) position, method, and approach.[21] For example, radically authoritarian and exclusivist theologians would nonetheless cite in their support the arguments of prestigious philosophers and verses of the great mystical poets; while strictly rationalist, even positivist philosophers would likewise articulate their positions using Qur'anic verses, sacred traditions, and ostensibly theological reasoning. Thus, within that shared range of literary background and vocabulary, educated readers were quickly trained to follow very carefully the *particular* arrangement and interconnection of arguments in the work at hand and especially to focus attentively on what was omitted (among a spectrum of possible counterarguments, refutations, etc.) and more subtly alluded to, as well as on what was openly cited and asserted.[22]

Ostad Elahi was an accomplished master of this traditional type of writing, trained from his youth in all the related religious and philosophical disciplines and literatures, and his normal expository procedure throughout *Knowing the Spirit*—even in the highly original chapter 7 at the heart of this work—is always the same. As such, the intended significance and distinctive innovative features of his approach would be immediately apparent to all his original readers versed in this tradition. That is, he typically begins with universal rational arguments, normally drawn from the repertoire of earlier Islamic philosophers; then he offers relatively subtle, but non-explicit allusions to the relevant spiritual phenomena; and eventually he concludes—above all in the latter half of chapter 7 here—with more explicit references to the mature fruit of his own direct spiritual observations, although still phrased in a relatively abstract metaphysical (rather than autobiographical or poetic) language.[23] Throughout this work it is important to note that the relevant scriptural sources, whether Qur'anic verses or teachings of the Shiite Imams, are provided at each stage as an ongoing additional support for these other, more explicitly universal forms of argument, and not as the sole or self-sufficient evidence.[24] Given this distinctive procedure, Ostad Elahi's original readers would immediately recognize the roots of his particular approach, with its distinctive emphasis on the development of his readers' *spiritual intelligence*—that is, on the rational, implicitly universal philosophical articulation of the distinctively spiritual dimensions of human being—as reflecting the philosophical school of Mulla Sadra, with its distinctive blending of Avicennan philosophical language with the unique spiritual and metaphysical issues and methods of the great figures and traditions of earlier Islamic "practical spirituality."[25]

However, those traditionally educated readers who did recognize the echoes of Mulla Sadra's language and thought in *Knowing the Spirit* would also immediately recognize, once they reached chapter 7, the relative novelty and originality of Ostad Elahi's far more explicit discussion of the different modalities of the process of spiritual perfection. This is especially the case with those particular modalities (especially the fourth item here) that would openly allow for the theologically sensitive notion of the possible "return" of imperfect human spirits to successive bodily forms on earth: here Ostad Elahi openly evokes a central, but intimately personal, dimension of human spiritual experience that even the famously outspoken Sufi poets had most often dealt with (in their *writing*, that is) only by way of allusion and symbolic expressions. At this point, confronted with the unexpectedly open and challenging evocation of actual spiritual experience and observations throughout chapter 7, thoughtful and probing readers from within this tradition would naturally return to explore the more subtle hints and allusions to that previously unsuspected dimension of spiritual reality that are in fact scattered throughout the opening chapters—and hopefully, to a deeper reconsideration of all the relevant, perhaps previously neglected, elements of their own spiritual experience. That is when the real process of reading and reflection would actually begin.

In this respect, it is particularly important to stress that *all* the formally eschatological sections of Ostad Elahi's book (chapters 3–8), regarding the "Return" and the destiny and perfection of the human spirit, are equally phrased in the form of an ostensibly third-person, external account of the proponents of various radically different understandings of this metaphysical process. This is not just a traditional literary form or a transparent device for masking the author's own opinions.[26] On the contrary, it is—to adapt his own central image from chapter 5—a very carefully constructed mirror to "capture the conscience" of each individual reader, to oblige each of us to reflect far more deeply and conscientiously about the actual grounds and deeper implications of our own spiritual understanding, beliefs, and experiences concerning this immensely important subject.[27]

Allusion and Realization

Knowing the Spirit is, as its author often reminds us, an extremely concise, summary treatment of what is in reality an unimaginably immense and complex subject, both existentially and philosophically. For each reader, the indispensable active connection between its formal arguments and familiar scriptural attestations and their eventual existential elaboration and illustration necessarily passes by way of

allusion (*ishāra*). And few dimensions of this tradition are more difficult to explain[28] to new readers coming from outside the tradition,
since what constitutes an effective allusion is so often dependent on
the readers' prior acquaintance with the familiar norms of the disciplines and language of the tradition in question, and on their resulting
implicit expectations. Incidentally, there is nothing particularly esoteric or mysterious about this *process* of allusion: we are all intimately
familiar with the multitude of ways that our everyday appreciation of
what we consider "good" poetry, music, or film (or even advertising!),
for example, is normally dependent on our ability to recognize what
is genuinely original and meaningful, and effectively "novel," in relation to earlier works of the same genre—and which thereby stands out
in contrast to the great mass of essentially repetitive, unoriginal imi-
tations. In the case of Ostad Elahi's work, the relevant background
assumed on the part of his original readers includes not only an informed acquaintance with the extensive earlier learned traditions of
Islamic philosophy and theology, but also with the near-universal
popular background of Persian spiritual *poetry*.[29] That immense tradition of spiritual teaching—itself thoroughly grounded in the teachings
and symbolic vocabulary of the Qur'an and hadith—also deals constantly with the central metaphysical and eschatological subjects of
Knowing the Spirit.[30]

Since a detailed explanation of the allusions in this work would
require a commentary much longer than the translated text itself, a
few basic examples will have to suffice. To begin with, certainly the
best starting point, as already mentioned, is to start by concentrating
on the connections between those short key passages (given in **bold
italics** here) that Ostad Elahi himself highlighted as an explicit key to
the intentions of this entire work.[31] Second, those particular passages,
whether longer or short, that initially appear to be somehow inconse-
quential or logically disconnected from the overall flow of their sur-
rounding context and argument are almost always intentionally
significant spiritual allusions that would immediately have stood out
as such for the original audiences of *Knowing the Spirit*. In chapter 1,
for example, during the succession of standard philosophical proofs
for the existence (and Attributes) of God, the fourth argument—from
"human beings' inability (to comprehend or explain) certain things
that happen to themselves. It includes such things as the sudden appearance of certain events that are extraordinary and supranatural,
whose reality cannot be denied"—suddenly confronts the reader with
an infinitely rich and open-ended domain of relevant spiritual experience, opening up perspectives that are quite indispensable for any

well-grounded understanding of the remaining eschatological chapters of this work.

Yet another illustration is Ostad Elahi's recurrent emphasis, throughout the initial philosophical sections of this work, on the considerations of divine *Justice* and *Wisdom* underlying the observed lawful regularity of the causal orders of being. Such vague philosophic expressions may at first seem like pious theological formulae, but they take on a much larger and unavoidably *existential* and practical (not just abstract theological) significance once the author has more openly reminded us—especially in chapter 7—of their implication in the alternative understandings of human beings' larger eschatological situation and destiny.[32] One final, and at least equally important, illustration is Ostad Elahi's brief analogy, near the end of chapter 3, of the process of spiritual perfection to the gradual, slowly cumulative process of human *education*. That is an allusion whose endless practical consequences and implications continue to unfold throughout every stage of the spiritual path, in ways comparable to Dante's *Divine Comedy*.

In general—and this may be the most practically useful and reassuring rule of thumb for readers new to this tradition—it is not really possible to be "mistaken" about any particular passage that seems to be a significant hint or allusion, however subtle or mysterious that initial intuition may be to us. That is to say, in a work of such extreme concision and density of expression, anything that momentarily obliges us to begin the real work of *active* reading—to question our assumptions, explore and revisit our intuitions, discover unexpected meanings and perspectives, or to probe for appropriate illustrations and implications: those are precisely the passages that deserve our closest attention and ongoing, probing reflection.

The Basic Structure of Knowing the Spirit: *The Origination and the Return*

The overall structure and order of treatment of the topics in this work, as both Ostad Elahi and his original readers were well aware, was taken over from a familiar, long-standing philosophical tradition going back to the famous Persian philosopher Avicenna (Ibn Sīnā, d. 428/1037), who systematically established the basic parallelism between traditional philosophical topics and Islamic theological issues and symbolism that has typified virtually all the subsequent schools of eastern Islamic philosophy and theology.[33] Within that wider metaphysical framework, *Knowing the Spirit* even more closely follows the highly abridged format and the distinctive philosophical content of a famous short eschatological treatise by Mulla Sadra, *The Wisdom of the Throne*.[34] Sadra's influential treatise summarizes the same initial onto-logical principles—above all, his distinctive vision of the universal "transubstantial movement" (*haraka jawhariyya*) of all creatures in their ultimate metaphysical "Return" to their divine Source of being (see chapters 1–3 in *Knowing the Spirit*)—while treating in the same order each of these alternative theological and philosophical understandings of the human spirit's perfection and Return. Sadra's work likewise culminates in an explicit emphasis on the indispensable role of the intermediate spiritual realm (the *barzakh*: chapter 7 here) in accounting for the wider, ongoing human process of spiritual perfection and in reconciling the different scriptural and theological allusions to that universal process of Return. As we have already noted, the parallels between the structure and progression of *Knowing the Spirit* and Sadra's earlier eschatological conceptions—more fully developed in his famous *Asfār* (*Book of the Four Spiritual Journeys*)—are so extensive that most of Ostad Elahi's original scholarly Persian readers would, at first read-ing, naturally observe that it is above all in the later sections of chapter 7 that he most openly expresses what are undeniably his own most original ideas and understandings. Or in other words, it is there (in chapter 7) that Ostad Elahi pointedly makes much more explicit and unambiguous these larger eschatological perspectives—above all, con-cerning the successive terrestrial lives of individual human spirits—that had prudently been phrased only as conceivable, implicit interpretive possibilities within the explicit metaphysical framework of Sadra's eschatological thought.

In addition, for readers approaching *Knowing the Spirit* without great familiarity with the Qur'an, it is also helpful to know that the parallelisms constantly assumed here between cosmological and eschatological themes—between symbolic accounts of the stages and creative processes of divine Self-manifestation, on the one hand, and the even more detailed symbolic descriptions of the spirit's pro-cess of purification, perfection, and ongoing Return—are absolutely central and explicit in the Qur'an, in ways that often make that rev-elation far more directly comparable with scriptures of eastern reli-gions than with the Bible as it is commonly read and understood today.[35] Not only are at least half the verses of the Qur'an explicitly connected with these intimately interrelated cosmological and eschatological processes,[36] but the remainder of the more practically oriented verses are only ultimately meaningful in relation to an ad-equate understanding of that wider metaphysical framework.[37] As such,

Ostad Elahi's work was composed—and originally intended to be read—against the widely accessible backdrop of centuries of highly developed traditions of both "theoretical" (i.e., philosophic and theological) and more practical spiritual approaches to the interpretation, understanding, and application of those central scriptural sources. So at the very least, new readers need to be aware that the elaborate equivalence assumed throughout *Knowing the Spirit* between, on the one hand, scriptural symbolism and theological discourse, and on the other hand the corresponding language and structures of earlier philosophy (i.e., ontology and epistemology) and paths of spiritual realization, does not originate with Ostad Elahi himself, but forms a familiar, integral part of wide-ranging literary and cultural traditions constantly shared by the author and his original learned audience.

Likewise, even the most "secular" modern reader needs to recognize the fundamental religious significance—and hence the heightened politico-theological sensitivity—of those alternative conceptions of human destiny and realization that Ostad Elahi passes in review in chapters 3 through 8 here. The answers that one eventually gives to these outwardly abstract and highly metaphysical questions in fact have unavoidable implications for central practical questions of right action, authority, guidance, and the wider ethical aims and reference points for each person's life in their wider community, not just for individual spiritual practice. To take one closely—perhaps inextricably—connected area of spiritual life that is scarcely even mentioned in *Knowing the Spirit*, all of Ostad Elahi's original readers would be profoundly aware that the existence of the "intermediate," spiritual world of the *barzakh* (developed here in chapters 5 and 7) is not simply related to the different eschatological possibilities and perspectives evoked in this short work. Throughout earlier Islamic spiritual traditions (and their parallels in other religions), that spiritual realm is universally understood as providing the metaphysical locus and theoretical underpinning for the immensely complex phenomenology of spiritual guidance and direction—that is, for the ongoing, invisible roles of the pleroma of higher spirits (the messengers, prophets, "friends of God," Imams, saints, and so on) in all the familiar spiritual realities and processes of prayer, dreams, guidance, intercession, communication, and the like that constitute the actual spiritual lives of human beings in every time and place.[38] Ostad Elahi does not have to mention explicitly that this immense, universal domain of human beings' actual spiritual life and practice is in reality absolutely inseparable from that larger eschatological "journey of spiritual perfection" (*sayr-i takāmul*) that forms the constant unifying theme of *Knowing the Spirit*.

Yet again, he leaves it to each of his readers to develop that practically indispensable connection.

III. The Contemporary Significance of *Knowing the Spirit*

Given what has just been explained about the compressed and intentionally allusive language and structure of *Knowing the Spirit*, one could readily describe the contemporary relevance of this work in the same terms Ostad Elahi applies here to each person's experience of the spiritual world (the *barzakh*) in chapter 5: it is "like a mirror: everyone sees their own form in it." Having admitted that, it may still be helpful to briefly mention—since any elaboration would quickly become a book in itself—a few of the salient issues and approaches taken up in this work that are likely to attract increasing attention in the future.[39]

To begin with, in an unavoidably global civilization marked by the constant collision and often the overt conflict of a multitude of once-separate cultural and spiritual traditions—a kind of increasingly chaotic dramatization of the tower of Babel—the distinctive phenomenologically based approach of spiritual research (*tahqīq*) or spiritual intelligence exemplified in *Knowing the Spirit*, along with Ostad Elahi's other writings, offers a remarkable potential for arriving at genuine understanding and creative, mutually cooperative responses to unavoidable human challenges, while respecting the inevitable diversity of spiritual perceptions and realizations. The consistently irenic approach that he applies here to the perennially disputed questions of eschatology and human destiny is potentially applicable to a much wider range of pervasive religious and cultural controversies.[40]

That is to say, rather than attempting to prove or impose a single "true" conception in this heatedly controversial domain—and thereby disprove and dismiss all other differing views—Ostad Elahi always begins, as in so many ways he also ends, with the actual irreducible phenomena: with a carefully nourished respect for the entire perennial range of individual spiritual experiences in this domain.[41] It is only on the basis of those common human realities—and always subject to further experiential testing and verification in that realm—that he gradually develops a series of wider metaphysical hypotheses, pointedly phrased in explicitly universal, rational terms, that can potentially account for the full spectrum of relevant experiences. Students of religion interested in the actual phenomenology of spiritual experience today—as well as the earlier beliefs and theologies of the different historical traditions—will of course be struck by the extraordinarily close convergence of Ostad Elahi's observations and four "modalities" of the process of spiritual development in chapter 7 here, at so many points, with the increasingly detailed range of relevant spiritual phenomena being brought forward in the burgeoning contemporary literatures on near-death experiences, hypnotic regression, and a wide range of practical therapeutic disciplines.[42]

Secondly, Ostad Elahi's ideas in *Knowing the Spirit*—especially his central conception of the ongoing transubstantial movement (*haraka jawhariyya*) of all of creation through that journey of spiritual perfection (*sayr-i takāmul*) constituting the cosmic process of Return—constantly refer to and help explain our common human experience of the central spiritual role of our intuitions regarding the wider *natural* world, a fundamental dimension of spirituality far too often neglected, at least in recent times, by many official representatives of the Abrahamic traditions, if not in the foundational scriptures themselves. Once again, this is an immense phenomenological field of spiritual experience and education commonly shared by all of humanity, in ways directly related to Ostad Elahi's distinctive approach of "spiritual research" whose prospects and promises were previously highlighted here.

Finally, Ostad Elahi's stress on the central role of the spiritual realm (the *barzakh*) in the ongoing process of spiritual perfection—which has close parallels in the spiritual teachings and practices of each of the world religious traditions—is a perspective whose "proof" and concrete reality is to be found, as he constantly illustrates throughout the thousands of anecdotes contained in *Athār al-Haqq*, precisely in the ongoing individual phenomena of the actual interrelations of the earthly and spiritual realms, including all the infinite personal manifestations of the spiritual pedagogy and guidance of those central spiritual figures (including, in the tradition he refers to here, the prophets and all the "Friends of God") whose realities are discovered in the course of each individual's unique spiritual practice and destiny. Here again, Ostad Elahi points to the ways the actual, endlessly diverse phenomena of our spiritual lives, when properly understood and appreciated, can become *complementary* revelations, guideposts, and invaluable lessons—rather than imagined "idols" of polemic opposition—along our intersecting paths to the common goal of spiritual perfection.

The Persian Text and Translation Conventions

The Persian Text

The edition of *Ma'rifat al-Rūh* used for this translation was the revised edition of 1992 (Tehran, Jayhūn, 1371 a.h.s.). I was able to consult directly with the editor, Dr. Bahram Elahi, for all questions concerning the edition and the original handwritten source of the printed text. In the original published edition, the editor placed at the end (in a short, separate section of "supporting texts") a number of extensive supporting Arabic quotations, from the Qur'an and other philosophical texts, which Ostad Elahi had originally included within the body of his manuscript.[1] In this translation, I have treated those annexed, supporting Arabic texts in *Knowing the Spirit* as follows. First, where the author originally provided the Arabic text of passages that he then translates into Persian, I have ordinarily given only *one* English translation, which is designed to convey all relevant nuances of the Arabic and Persian alike. This includes the vast majority of the supporting texts. In other cases, where the supporting textual material was original and helpful in understanding Ostad Elahi's arguments, I have actually translated the entire item in a note where it was originally situated. Finally, three longer Arabic supporting texts, which cite at length traditional theological and philosophical disputations that would only interest specialists in this field (who in any case are already able to access the original printed text directly), have simply been summarized and identified in the corresponding notes.

Translation Conventions

This translation follows certain standard scholarly conventions in translations from Persian and Arabic texts. In particular, regular parentheses are often used to indicate short additions of English words—not literally given in the original language—that are actually needed to give a more normal English reading. Given that usage, I have carefully avoided parentheses (using dashes instead) to translate any of the author's own parenthetical remarks. On the other hand, square brackets are used to indicate any *additional* explanations that have actually been added by the translator. This usage extends to endnotes: all notes (or partial additions) given here in square brackets have been added by the translator.

All translations of Qur'anic passages are provided by the translator and are consistently given in italics in this translation. Qur'an references are identified by the numbers of the corresponding sura and verse (e.g., 1:4). Readers who happen to compare these translations with most commercial versions in English should be reassured that almost all the "eschatological" verses in the Qur'an actually emphasize, in the original Arabic, the *presence* of the spiritual realities concerned. They are usually in the present continuous tense, not the explicitly temporal future (which is stressed and indicated as such by a relatively rare explicit grammatical marker). There are many other common features of available Qur'an translation in Western languages that likewise profoundly distort and misrepresent the Arabic meanings of key eschatological terms.[2]

One of the characteristic features of the traditional scholarly Persian prose writing style used by Ostad Elahi in *Knowing the Spirit* is the frequent insertion of short, non-Qur'anic Arabic quotations—of proverbs, philosophical terms, technical expressions, and so on—in ways that resemble the frequent citation of comparable Latin, Greek, and even Hebrew phrases in learned Western vernacular prose contexts (whether in English or other European languages) prior to the later twentieth century. In general, I have simply given translations of all such short Arabic quotations, including hadith, between quotation marks, but without the italics reserved here for Qur'anic quotations alone.

As already indicated, the author's own intentionally underlined, important passages in the original manuscript, pointedly highlighting his personal emphases and key philosophical contributions, have been given in this translation—as was already the case in the original Persian published edition—in *italic boldface*. All other italics (apart from Qur'anic passages) are due to the translator, usually attempting to suggest particular emphases implicit in the original Persian.

The original textual sources for all other works cited in the original notes here are listed in the initial author's references section of the bibliography at the end of this translation. Following scholarly conventions, book titles in Arabic (even for Persian works) and Arabic names of unfamiliar earlier scholars have been transliterated according to a simplified version of the standard (IJMES/Library of Congress) Arabic transliteration system, eliminating the diacritical points under certain consonants. Names of more recent or contemporary Iranian writers have been given simply according to the particular forms they have adopted for use in Latin scripts. Where certain proper names or technical terms have become familiar in English usage (e.g., Avicenna, Mulla Sadra, Ostad Elahi, Hafez, Saadi), they have normally been given in those standard anglicized forms, without transliteration.

Knowing the Spirit

Original Table of Contents

Knowing the Spirit

- An allusion to the falsity of a vicious circle or infinite regression of causes: this establishes an original Cause of causes, which is the Eternal, the Necessary Being by Its Essence; and that everything else that exists comes into being through the effusion of the grace of His Self-emanation, according to the laws of cause and effect.

Second Argument [the teleological argument], from the ordered structures of change among all creatures, and from the necessary requirements of the essential natures of all existents:

- Moving from effects to their Cause: the saying of Imam Ali (on the "effects of the Eternal One") and verses from sura 88 of the Qur'an.

Third Argument [the cosmological need for an Ultimate Cause of nature], refuting the arguments of the materialists and the naturalists, by showing the false consequences of their opinions:

- First, no nature can be the cause for the existence of its own nature.

- Second, several natures cannot be the causes of each other at the same moment.

- Third, if all the natures at the different levels of the chain (of existentiating causality) are the causes of the existence of what is below them, without any end, that necessarily entails an infinite regression of causes (which is false).

- (Therefore in reality) the nature (of each existent thing) has its (ultimate) Source in its relation to the Necessary Being by Essence.

- (The division of all existent things into) the natural and the artificial, and (their further subdivision) into what is regularly ordered and irregular.

Fourth Argument, from the inability of human beings (to comprehend) certain realities connected with themselves or other supranatural happenings:

Fifth Argument, from the contingency of all things (in relation to) the Eternal:

- (Arguments from) the changeability of the world, and from the composite nature of all bodies.

- That the (scriptural) expression *"eternally,"* in respect to the creatures (in the spiritual world of the Return), is relative (unlike God's absolute Eternity).

How the Return takes place, according to (the proponents of) the process of spiritual perfection, including four modalities:

First modality: **the process of perfection by "transposition"** from the material world to the intermediate (spiritual) world

- The intermediate world (*barzakh*).

- That the intermediate world has also been metaphorically termed the "imaginal" world or "world of likenesses."

- Arguments from religious tradition supporting the existence of the intermediate world, from the Qur'an, Ja'far al-Sādiq, and (sayings of the Imams in) *Majma' al-Bahrayn*.

Second modality: **the process of perfection through a "connection"** between the intermediate world and the material world

Third modality: **the process of perfection through "accumulation"** (of the different influences of minerals, plants and animals) during the arc of spiritual ascent

First, the continuous transubstantial movement (of all creatures) through the arc of spiritual ascent.

Second, that this (universal) ascending movement takes place by means of changes that are continuously ongoing and in the same place.

  - Kumayl's questioning Imam Ali and his enumerating the four kinds of souls.

Third, that when the time comes for the dissolution of the material vital force of minerals, plants, and animals (at death), those material constituents return to the basic mineral elements of the earth.

Fourth Modality: **the "unitive" process of perfection,** by means of the two arcs of ascent and descent:

- The likening of the spirit to "wind" or "breath."

- People with a "body of clay, spirit of clay" (lacking the angelic spirit).

- The moment of the inbreathing of the (angelic) spirit and its uniting with the body, according to Qur'anic verses.

- One thousand and one spiritual stages have been established for the perfection of the human spirit.

- The essential differences between the unitive process of spiritual perfection and the (false) ideas of the transmigrationists.

[Other topics connected with the unitive process of spiritual perfection]:

1. The maximum allotted period for (each human spirit's) passing through all the stages of spiritual perfection is *fifty thousand years.*

2. The average lifetime of each human bodily form is considered fifty years.

3. If one's lifespan is longer than that in one human body, then it will be shorter in other lifetimes.

4. The period of fifty thousand years allows for a thousand human lifetimes.

5. A newborn baby must live more than forty days in order for that life to be counted as one (of that spirit's allotted human) lifetimes.

6. If a spirit is obliged to descend into a nonhuman bodily form [as a special punishment], that period is not counted in its allotted fifty thousand years.

7. If a spirit has not completed its thousand spiritual stages of perfection after its allotted fifty thousand years, then it will remain forever deprived of the grace of (the spiritual rank of) perfection, and it will enter the eternal paradise or Gehenna.

8. Each time that a person dies, the body disintegrates and their spirit is transferred to the intermediate world for a certain time.

9. The length of time a spirit remains in the intermediate world is not the same for everyone.

10. "Garment for garment," "turn for turn" (and other expressions alluding to the process of spiritual perfection).

11. That the creatures on the planet earth are either masculine, feminine, or in between.

12. The "demotion" of a human spirit [in the rare cases of a special punishment] is only through a (temporary) connection with those animals possessing the power of reflection.

13. The cases of "intruding" (exchanged) spirits and "apparitional" spirits, as mentioned in the Qur'an.

14. The inequalities and injustices in each (human) creature's life are the results of their past, present, and future actions.

15. Why (the embodied human spirit ordinarily) forgets the memories of its previous human lives:

   • First explanation: the density of the obscuring dust of its bodily matter and the passions of its (lower, human-animal) soul.

   • Second explanation: if its previous lives were not forgotten, the spirit would be judged as though it had only one single lifetime, which means its allotted period of "proof" (for gradually reaching perfection) would not really exist.

   • Third explanation: if spirits didn't forget their previous lives, that would lead to the breakdown of the social order (because of the intensity of remembered grievances and attachments).

Three exceptional cases in which (some of a person's) previous human lives are *not* forgotten:

   • First exception: newborn children, for at least forty days, and often somewhat longer.

   • Second exception: when a human spirit is placed [by way of a temporary punishment] in connection with an animal form.

   • Third exception: Human beings with exceptional spiritual antecedents (in previous lives), who have now become liberated from attachments to this world and who have gained control over their (human-animal) soul.

An Illuminating Remark: concerning the rewards and punishments for good and bad actions:

First, (our earthly actions have *both*) their consequences in this world and their rewards or punishments in the other (spiritual) world.

Second, good actions are rewarded ten times over, while bad deeds receive only a single, equivalent punishment, (as indicated in) the Qur'anic verse (6:160).

Third, that the distinctive qualities and quantities of the pleasures and pains actually occurring in the eternal realm of the Return are indescribable.

Fourth, that the "eternal" punishments (mentioned by the scriptures) in the other world (only take place) when (each human spirit's) allotted period of "proof" in this world has been completed.

Introduction

This is the Book *Knowing the Spirit*

In the Name of God, the All-Loving, the All-Merciful[1]

Praise be to God, the Lord of the worlds, Who is *All-Loving* and *All-Merciful*! All praises to *the Master of the Day of Judgment*, Who is both Ruler and All-Wise! And glory to God Almighty, Who is *the Unique* and the Chief! Praise be to God the All-Powerful, Who is *Sempiternal* and Upright! All blessings be upon that Essential Reality *Which does not engender and is not engendered*, Who is All-Living and Eternal! All thanks to the Creator of all creatures, *Who has no peer and is All-Generous*! All worship to the Necessary Being, Who is All-Hearing and All-Knowing! And all supplication to the absolutely Able, Who is Most Glorious and Most Supreme! All help is from God the Exalted, from Whom is *the Straight Path*; all refuge is with the Most *Noble of those who record* (82:11), Who gives the Gardens (of paradise) to the good as their just reward, and to the bad (the torments of) the Fire.

May (God's) blessings and peace and endless praises be upon all the prophets and all *the friends of God* (10:62) and *those drawn near* (56:11) to Him, especially Muhammad and the leaders (Imams) of right guidance!

As for the rest, this humble servant, Nur Ali Elahi, begins by saying that a group of friends have kept on asking me to write down what was alluded to—but not fully developed—concerning the problem of knowing the spirit at the end of (my book) *The Demonstration of the Truth*.[2] So out of respect for them and their request, and in accordance with my religious duty, I was obliged to undertake this task, since *properly responding to the religious requests of those who are following a path of spiritual guidance is among the basic religious responsibilities*.[3]

39

That is why, God willing, I will explain this subject here as far as I have understood it and to the extent of what needs to be said, for the sake of guiding this human community. It is obvious that only God truly knows the accuracy and inaccuracy of all this, so (as the proverb has it): "whatever strange things may reach your ears, at least consider them to be in the realm of what is possible."[4] To begin with, we must recall that it is necessary to make allowances for some of the shortcomings and defects of this composition, given the following special difficulties:

1. The true reality of this matter is so complex and profound that no one would ever claim to have perfectly understood the complete truth about this subject to the degree it deserves, unless it be the prophets sent (by God) and those drawn near to the Supreme Station (of proximity to God)—and each of them has only been inspired to the extent of what God considered appropriate. So all that can be said is that "each person has only understood the matter within the limits of their own understanding." Or in the words of Shaykh Saadi:

Those who pretend to know about This are really ignorant.

> For the person who *has* learned something about It will
> not be heard from![5]

2. The majority of minds will not be able to comprehend many of these subjects, nor will they all be easy for most ears to accept— even to the extent that they can be supported by religious traditions, or can be grasped by arguments and reasonings within the limits of the intellect, or have become clear for certain individuals as a result of their special proximity to God, through the unveiling of the mysteries of the divine realities. That is why, for the spiritual elite, these subjects are considered part of (God's) "hidden secrets."

3. Whatever I would like to set forth here is still restricted by the limited capacity of my thinking, the incompleteness of my understanding, the shortcomings of my perception, and the partial extent of my information. So it is possible that it might not seem adequate for some intellectuals, which would be regrettable.

Our goal, which is truly knowing the spirit, requires the following (steps):

- First, to come to know the *Creator* of the spirit, so that we may discover the Source of the spirit's existence.

- Second, to define the spirit, so that we can know who it is, what are the qualities of its essential nature, and what are its specific defining characteristics.

- Third, to establish the *immortality* of the spirit, so that we can establish its returning[6] (to God) in the realm of the Return.[7] Otherwise, the reality of the returning and the realm of the Return could not be proved.

- Fourth, (to set forth) the subject of the "Gathering" and "Reawakening" (of the spirits) in the physical and the spiritual Returning and the right combination of those two, in order to eliminate certain illusions and misunderstandings that are prevalent among both ordinary people and the (learned) elite in regard to this subject.

Of course in regard to each of these above-mentioned matters, what needs to be said has already been proclaimed by the prophets sent as messengers by the order of *the Lord of the worlds* (1:2) in order to awaken the creatures of this planet Earth, through their mentioning various arguments and proofs, supported by *clear Signs/verses* (24:34, etc.)—including both universal and particular (arguments) and universals and particulars[8]—which do not need any further explanation. However, here we will set forth in the following chapters, by way of reconciling all those different accounts, a summary of their extensive explanations and an overview of their detailed statements, in order to enlighten the understanding of those who are traveling the spiritual Path.

Chapter One

Establishing the Existence of the Divine Artisan

A great many arguments and proofs establishing the existence of the divine Artisan and Lord of the worlds, as well as sure signs and evidences of the unicity of the Unique and Majestic Creator, have been set forth in the sacred scriptures as well as in the works of scholars, mystics, philosophers, and theologians, encompassing arguments based on (religious) tradition, the intellect, the sciences, and philosophy. However in this book, which follows a summary approach, we must forgo a detailed exposition of all those works and limit ourselves to mentioning certain arguments based on tradition, the intellect, and the evidence of the senses. We hope this will prove acceptable to our esteemed readers.

First Argument
[for the "Necessary Being"]:

It is postulated that everything conceivable must fall under one of the following three modes: that which is *necessary*, that which is *impossible*, and that which is *possible*. Each of those modes includes the following further subdivisions:

1. That which is necessary in virtue of itself; that which is necessary through another; and that which is necessary by relation to another.

43

2. That which is impossible in virtue of itself; that which is impossible through another; and that which is impossible by relation to another.

3. That which is possible in virtue of itself; that which is possible by relation to another.

The definition of each of those three modes is as follows:[1]

A. What is *necessary by virtue of itself* refers to that whose being is necessary by virtue of itself. This means that each of the different kinds of essential nonexistence—whether preceding it, or as its concomitant, or imaginary—is logically and really impossible with regard to its being: an example is the being of the Creator. This mode is called "necessary by virtue of itself." So everything else that exists is "necessary through another" or "necessary in relation to another," in that (its existence) goes back in the end to this (Creator or Source which is) "necessary by essence." For those beings that come into being through another by the intermediary of primary and secondary causes, as well as those beings that are necessarily brought into existence through a relation which is analogous to that of being brought into being through another[2]—in other words, the whole field of primary and secondary causes caused by another or through relation to another: all of these go back in the end to the original Cause of causes, which is necessary by virtue of Itself, the Essence of the Necessary Being.

B. What is *impossible by virtue of itself*, as opposed to what is necessary by virtue of itself, is that whose nonexistence is necessary in itself. In other words, none of the different kinds of existence by virtue of itself—whether preceding it, as an essential concomitant, or in imagination—are in any way applicable to it. An example (of this kind of impossibility) is the existence of a partner for the Creator (i.e., another "God" exactly like the Creator). This mode is what is called "that whose existence is impossible by virtue of itself." All the other impossible things, including what is "impossible through another" or "impossible by relation to another," also come back in the end to this (i.e., to what is impossible in itself).

C. What is *possible by virtue of itself* is that which, in itself, is not necessarily or preponderantly either necessary or impossible. So there is no determining factor (as to whether it is either necessary or impossible) intrinsic to itself. In other words, since the two sides (of its necessity or impossibility) are equal and it is intrinsically in need (of another external causal factor to determine whether it is necessary or impossible), the deciding factor in either direction must be caused by an external preponderating cause that moves it in one direction or the other (i.e., toward that whose existence is either necessary or impossible).

(Furthermore), if necessity is excluded with regard to only one side (i.e., if something is said to be either "not-impossible" or "not-necessary"), that is called "general possibility." And if necessity is excluded with regard to both sides, that is called "particular possibility." But if all of the forms of necessity are excluded—whether essential, descriptive, or temporal—then that case is termed "the most particular possibility." In addition, "possibility by potentiality" and "possibility by receptivity" are also considered among the divisions of possible things.

Indeed the mode of what is "possible through another" is not really intelligible, because the notion of something as "possible by virtue of itself" is an inherent quality that is inferred from the very quiddity[3] of that (possible) thing, by considering its need for an external primary or secondary cause to determine whether it will either exist or be impossible. Since the inferring of that quality (of a quiddity being "possible by virtue of itself") is based on the essence of the quiddity (of that possible thing) by itself, there is no need to consider any additional mediating element beyond that essence. Thus the notion of something being "possible through another" is rationally pointless, since the essential qualities of things don't need any external cause. Moreover, (to consider) a particular quiddity as being "possible through another," when it is (already) intrinsically "possible by virtue of itself," is self-contradictory and would mean combining two contrary qualities in its regard.

Of course each of these three basic modes has been the subject of lengthy philosophic discussions, but to enter into those discussions in detail would take us beyond the limits of this intentionally summary work. Therefore, as we have just indicated, each thing that is either necessary or impossible through another or through its relation to another, or else possible through relation to another, must eventually go back in the end to an ultimate Cause of causes. Otherwise it would necessarily lead to either a circle (of mutual causation) or an infinite chain of causes, and it is a basic logical principle that both those notions are absurd and incorrect.[4]

Given the absurdity of a circle or infinite chain of causation, we must look for an *original* Cause of causes. According to both the intellect and the voice of conscience, there must be Something that is not caused by any cause; that is not determined by any (other) power nor brought about by anything external; that is not composite through any mixture of components; that does not arise through any material substrate; that is not bound by any quiddity; that exists by Itself without any (other cause for its) being; whose existence does not depend on matter and form;[5] that cannot be qualified by any attributes other

(than Its own); that cannot be encompassed by any container nor de-
limited by any dimension or limit. Likewise, a beginning or end must
not be attributed to It, such that the mind might imagine Its being
prior or posterior (and thus limited by time). Nor must It be said to
have any partner or peer, since that would be a cause for association
and duality, for opposition or contradiction with regard to the connection between Its Willing and the direction and proper ordering of all
the creatures.

Thus as it says in the Qur'an: *If there were to be in the two of them*
[the heavens and the earth] *gods other than the* (One) *God, then both of*
them would be destroyed. . . . (21:22). Hence as a general rule His Perfection must be whole and complete in every possible respect, to the
greatest possible degree and extent, and His Being must be free from
every weakness and defect. Whatever name may be given to such a
One is permissible, and accordingly some call Him "the Creator," others
"God," others "the Essentially Necessary Being," and so on.

In any case, everything that exists comes from the effusions of
the bountiful Grace of His overflowing Self-emanation, which brings
into being all the existent things with their harmonious, well-balanced
gradations of distance and proximity (to Him), of intensity and weakness, and their interrelations of ultimate and secondary causes and
effects. In other words, from the highest stage of the very first (divine)
emanation, the First Intelligence, on down to the weakest and lowliest
of the creatures, every one of the possible things is brought into the
field of actual existence and takes on its being through a secondary
(proximate) and an ultimate cause (which all go back ultimately to
that One Cause of causes).

Second Argument
[(the teleological or cosmological argument) from the ordered
structures of change among all creatures, and from the necessary
requirements of the essential natures of all existents]:[6]

The second argument (for the existence of a divine Artisan/Creator)
comes from observing the ordered structures of all the creatures and
the specific requirements of the natures of all existing beings. As can
be observed directly through our senses, every thing has by design a
beginning and an end, (distinctive) movements and limits, a regularly
ordered arrangement of effects and influences, and an ordered, systematic structure—all such that at no time and place do we find any
intrinsic[7] failure or defect (in this natural order of nature).

Therefore anyone with a sound intellect who carefully observes
those specific natural orders and structures will be certain that these

circumstances and conditions—with their vast extent and ingenuity, their great power and influences, combined with such guiding thought and extraordinary originality—have not come into being by themselves or through something of the same order as themselves. For nothing that is itself caused[8] can be the ultimate cause of itself or the ultimate cause of other caused things of the same order as itself. For example, a statue is not capable of creating itself, nor can any other statue like it be capable of creating it. Therefore every caused thing must come into existence through a cause higher than itself, and everything that is made must come into existence through a maker higher than itself.

So all of these regularly ordered structures in the different areas of existence firmly establish that there is a Bestower of being, a Managing and Ordering Force, for the universe and its inhabitants, and for the natural phenomena of generation and destruction.

In general, we must come to recognize the Source of those effects (in all the ordered structures of nature) through observing those effects, as was indicated in the following saying of Ali:[9]

> Someone asked the Imam Ali about establishing the existence of a divine Artisan, and he replied: "Camel-droppings point to the existence of a camel, and the donkey's to the existence of a donkey, just as footsteps in the ground point to the existence of someone who was walking there. So that lofty and graceful temple of the heavens, or the lower center (of the levels of this world) in all its density—how can they not point to (the existence of God) the *All-Pervading* and *All-Knowing*?!" Then he said: "The works of God are signs pointing to His existence, and through our intellects we can come to believe in and know Him; by thoughtfully reflecting (on those signs) we can confirm the proof (of His Presence). He is knowable through the signs (of His Handiwork) and openly manifest through His *clear Signs*."[10]

In support of Ali's saying that the ordered structure (of the heavens) on high and the center (of the earth) below are reminders of God's Creation, there are numerous allusions to this in the Qur'an itself. Among them are the following verses:

> *Do you all not regard the camels, how they were created? And the heavens, how they were raised up? And the mountains, how they were set up? And the earth, how it was stretched out? Therefore reflect and remember, for you are only (here) to reflect and remember—you are not in control over them!* (88:17–22)

Third Argument [(the need for an Ultimate Cause of nature),
refuting the arguments of the materialists and the naturalists by
showing the false consequences of their opinions]:

According to the opinion of the materialists and the naturalists,[11] what
brings into being the nature of each thing is precisely nature itself. But
that view has many false consequences, including the following points:

1. To begin with, if each nature is itself what brings its own
   nature into being, then that would imply that that thing would
   have to exist prior to itself, which is false.

2. Second, if two or more natures are causing each other, within
   a limited situation and at the same time, then that would imply
   a vicious circle (of mutually existentiating causation), whether
   openly or implicitly—and that is not possible.

3. Third, if all the different natures at the different levels of the
   chain (of "vertical," existentiating causality) were infinite, with
   each one causing the existence of the nature beneath it, yet
   without ever reaching an (original causal) point that gives
   existence to the nature of all the natures, then that would
   imply an infinite regression of causes—and that supposition is
   also clearly false. In other words, if the (causal) effect of the
   different natures upon each other (can only be explained) by
   means of a vicious circle or an infinite regression, that (hy-
   pothesis) must be rejected. And if instead we must reach an
   ultimate (causal) Point above nature, then that is just the right
   answer. For that ultimate, highest Point of Unicity, which gives
   being to all that exists, *is* the divine Artisan, whatever name
   we may give It.

Hence what the materialists (and naturalists) referred to as "Nature"—that is, a nature without any Cause for its existence, an ultimate preponderance for existence (rather than nonexistence) without
any preponderating Cause for that[12]—is simply mistaken. Instead
nature—whether that be nature as a whole or each particular, relative nature—is an effect among the various potential effects of creation and a secondary cause among all the secondary causes brought
into actual existence by the Giver of existence. Thus nature finds its
original Source in the effusions of the bountiful Grace of the overflowing Self-emanation of the Creator of all the natures and in the
being of the essentially Necessary Being. So to put it simply, this

meaning of "nature" is the opposite of what the materialists meant by that term!

Now the existence of every existent thing must come to be either by nature or "artificially."[13] In either of those cases it can be either "regularly ordered" or "irregular," as explained below:

1. A "regularly ordered natural" existent comes to exist, through the intermediary of a natural potential, as an actualized form with a regular, intelligible order. Such things include the orbits of the planets; the motions of the stars, both fixed or changing; the shapes, colors, well-ordered bodily frames, structures, and dimensions of both animate and inanimate creatures; and so on.

2. An "irregular natural" existent is the contrary of a regularly ordered natural one. Such things include the relative height or lowness of the earth and its hills, the surging of springs and the flowing course of rivers, the uninhabited deserts and seashores, wild plants in the desert, trees in the forests, and so on.

3. A "regularly ordered artificial/intentional" existent is one whose regular intelligible order has come about through another factor in addition to the actual and potential influences of nature. That influence is the factor of a prior guiding volition and plan, according to a specific, intelligible principle or formula. Such things include the mathematical engineering of buildings, bridges, landscape design, fields and gardens, pools, masonry, and so on.

4. An "irregular artificial/intentional" existent is one in which the intentionally ordering factor of that prior guiding volition and plan is purposefully carried out in an irregular natural form, for a particular aesthetic goal and specific purpose. Such things include the arts and crafts imitating irregular natural phenomena, and other things.

Fourth Argument
[from the inability of human beings (to comprehend)
certain realities connected with themselves or other
supranatural happenings]:

This argument[14] flows from human beings' inability (to comprehend or explain) certain things that happen to themselves. It includes such things as the sudden appearance of certain events that are extraordinary and supranatural, whose reality cannot be denied, but which are unexpected and inexplicable during certain (historical) periods, such as miracles and other things.

Fifth Argument
[from the contingency of all things in relation to the Eternal]:

This is based on the situation of the eternity or contingency[15] of things. For everything that we can conceive must be either eternal (from the very beginning), or else contingent (coming into existence in time). Now we can visibly see and realize that all external (physical) and mental existents have been, are, and will be contingent. That is expressed in the following (classical examples) of the lesser and greater premises of a first-form syllogism in logic:

> The world is subject to change.
>   Everything subject to change is contingent.
>   Therefore: the world is contingent.

And also:

> All bodies are composite.
>   Everything composite is contingent.
>   Therefore: all bodies are contingent.[16]

Thus everything that is contingent (that comes into existence) must inevitably have some agent that brings it into existence. Now supposing that that agent must itself be brought into existence by another agent (and so on), then in the end we're brought back to an ultimate Cause and Bringer-into-existence, Who must be absolutely Eternal. For otherwise, (the lack of any ultimate Cause) would entail a vicious circle (of mutual causality) or an infinite chain of causes—and both (those alternatives), as has already been mentioned, are false and absurd.

As a consequence of this, the being of the Creator must be pre-Eternal and all the other existents must be brought into existence through Him. Hence in the Qur'an the process of reasoning of the prophet Abraham, the intimate friend of God, bears witness to this same argument, where it says:

> *And thus We caused Abraham to see* (God's) *Rulership of the heavens and the earth, that he might be among those having*

certainty. So when the night covered him over, he saw a star; he said: "This is my Lord." But when it went down he said: "I do not love those things that go down." Then when he saw the moon rising, he said: "This is my Lord." But when it went down, he said: "If my Lord does not guide me rightly, surely I shall be among those who go astray!" Then when he saw the sun rising, he said: "This is my Lord—this is greater!" But when the sun set, he said: "O my people, verily I am innocent of that which you are associating (with God). *Surely I have turned my face toward the One-Who-Originates the heavens and the earth, in pure faith; nor am I among those who associate* (any other with God)*!"* (6:75–79)

Now it is clear from the context of these verses that the prophet Abraham, in describing his seeing the rising and setting of the star, moon, and sun, did not mean to imply that he didn't recognize that God was One, nor that he himself somehow needed to learn and confirm that conception. On the contrary, faced with a people who were worshipping stars and the moon and the sun, he established a process of argument intended to awaken and enlighten them and to teach them a spiritual lesson, by refuting (their mistaken views) and trying to help them to inquire for themselves and to seek to understand.

Indeed for every thing, passing away and disappearing are necessary concomitants of its changing and coming to be. And every contingent being is also created. So only the divine Artisan is truly pre-Eternal and Everlasting. That is just (what is expressed) in the following report[17] transmitted by 'Alī Ibn Muhammad Ibn al-Juham, who said:

> I was at a gathering of (the Abbasid caliph) al-Ma'mūn, and Imam Reza was also there with him. Ma'mūn asked Imam Reza: "O son[18] of the Prophet, haven't you said that the prophets were all divinely protected from error?"
>
> Imam Reza replied: "Yes indeed!"
>
> Then Ma'mūn continued questioning him about passages from the Qur'an concerning the prophets, and he asked him: "Tell me about God's saying with regard to Abraham: *Then when the night covered him over* . . . (at 6:76–79)."
>
> In response to Ma'mūn, Imam Reza said: "The occasion for these verses was the time when the prophet Abraham came out of his hiding place and addressed himself to three groups: those who worshipped the Venus, the

moon, and the sun. It is because of this, following the orders
of his most generous Lord, that the prophet Abraham
pointed out the rising and setting of that star and the moon
and the sun so as to establish the falsity of the beliefs of
these three groups: that is, in order to encourage them to
inquire for themselves, question (their beliefs), and seek to
understand—not simply in order to inform or to show them
(the observable physical phenomena). . . . As he says (at the
end of this passage in the Qur'an): it is not appropriate to
worship and serve the likes of the sun and moon and stars.
It is only right to worship and serve their Creator, the Creator of the heavens and the earth. Therefore what the
prophet Abraham brought here as a "decisive Proof" (*hujja*)
against his people was an inspiration that God sent to him,
according to God's saying (at 6:83): *That is Our Proof which
We brought to Abraham against his people.* . . .

Ma'mūn said: "May God bless you abundantly, O son
of the Prophet!"

In addition, there is another saying transmitted from Imam Reza[19]
concerning the problem of the Eternal and the contingent—[in response
to the caliph al-Ma'mūn's questioning him about the meaning of the
following Qur'anic verse: *He it is Who created the heavens and the earth
in six Days, while His Throne was upon the Water, so that He might try you
all, which of you is best in works.* . . . (11:7)]—in which he says:

God Almighty created the Throne and the Water and the
angels *before* He created the heavens and the earth. The
angels took themselves and the Throne and Water as signs
pointing to the existence of the divine Artisan. Then He
placed the Throne over the Water in order to demonstrate
His Power to the angels, so that they might know that He
has power over every thing (42:39; 46:33). Then He raised up
the Throne through His Power and transported it and placed
it above the seven heavens, and *He created the heavens and
the earth in six Days.*

Now God had absolute power over His Throne and
was able to create all the heavens and earth in the blink of
an eye. But He created them over six Days in order to show
the angels that He creates things gradually, one thing after
the other. This was so the angels could infer (from this) that
the manifestation of everything that comes into existence,

one moment after another, is (only) through the being of the Maker, may He be exalted!

Nor did God create the Throne out of any need for it, since *He is Self-sufficient*, free from any need for the Throne or any other creature. Nor should He be described as being (literally) "on" the Throne, since He is not a body—and He is far, far exalted above being described by any attributes of His creation.[20]

And as for His saying *so that He might try you all, which of you is best in works* (11:7), that means that He created the creatures so that He could test them with regard to their fulfilling the duties of obedience and worship and service—not in order to investigate or experiment (with them), since God is already *Knowing of every thing* (33:40, etc.).

Then (the caliph) Ma'mūn said: "You have resolved my problem, O Abū al-Hasan (Imam Reza)—May God also resolve yours!"

Finally, Shaykh Amīr, one of the great figures of (the spiritual order of) the People of the Truth, also composed a short rhymed summary of this topic of contingency and the Eternal in Kurdish. Here is an explanation of that poem:[21]

We are travelers on the path of coming into being (*hudūth* = H), traveling toward Eternity (*qidam* = Q). "Coming into being" consists in the gradual bringing into existence of the creatures throughout the course of the temporal and spatial movements of the process of spiritual perfection.[22] Only God, the Everlasting, can be Eternal, He Who was before anything was and Who will exist forever.

For our coming into being is not through ourselves—as the materialists have imagined—but rather *through the blessings of the Will* and the Power of (One Who is) *Self-subsistent* and *All-Powerful, All-Living* and *Eternal*, the (One Who is) truly *King*—Who is *Lord of the Worlds* and will be *Master of the Day of Judgment* (1:1–2). He is *the Master of silk-weaving* in the sense that through the rules *of the covenant* of the silk-loom of nature, by means of the *disciples* of cause-and-effect, He gradually weaves one thing after another and continually sustains *the warp and weft* of His creation.

For the flawless *Design* of the intrinsic orders of all the creatures of the universe is *woven out* from the effusions of the emanation of God's all-sustaining *Loving-kindness* and His overflowing *Grace*. So we, who are the creations of that Creator, must be *faithful to that Pact* and that eternal *Covenant*. We must *weave speedily* on the warp and weft of (our own) process of spiritual perfection leading to reunion with the full Perfection of that Source of all Reality, for "Everything returns to its Source."[23]

Indeed Shaykh Amir, in this short summary, has managed to include the Eternity of the Creator, the contingency of all the creatures, the Covenant of *"Am I not your Lord?,"*[24] as well as the stages of the path and the process of spiritual perfection.

This is enough of chapter 1, devoted to establishing the existence of the divine Artisan, for those readers who have wisdom and spiritual insight. With God's help, let us begin chapter 2.

Chapter Two

The Spirit

Part One: The Definition of the Spirit, or the Rational Soul

Here is a comprehensive definition of the spirit (*ruh*), drawn together from the contents of the interpretation of the Qur'an, the declarations of the Imams, and the teachings of the religious scholars, philosophers, and theologians. The spirit, or "rational soul,"[1] is that which is the life-source for each being; the origin of the different distinctive perceptions and powers of action and reaction; the originating basis for all natural forms; and the governor and director of all the forms of organization in the substrates of being and quiddity, matter and form, and the nature and specific constitution of every existent thing. According to another source,[2] it has also been said that "the spirit is a subtle substance that pervades the physical body just as water circulates through a flower, oil through sesame seeds, or as fire passes through burning charcoal and light passes through the air."

Part Two: How the Spirit Was Created

There are a great many rational arguments and scriptural testimonies concerning the way the spirit was created. In particular, there are the numerous verses (on this subject) in the Qur'an, and there exist many soundly transmitted reports among the sayings and traditions of the Imams. However, since this book is meant to be a summary, we must limit ourselves to mentioning the following Qur'anic verses and sayings (from the Imams).

Qur'anic Verses[3]

1. *Surely the Messiah, Jesus the son of Mary, is the messenger of God and His Word that He placed within Mary, and a spirit from Him . . . (4:171)*

2. *And when your Lord said to the angels: "Verily I am creating a human-animal (bashar) from earth, from foul-smelling mud. So when I have rightly shaped him and I have breathed into him from My spirit, then you all bow down to him, prostrating yourselves." (15:28–29)*

3. *And they are asking you about the spirit. Say: "The spirit is from my Lord's Command, and you all have only been given a little knowledge." (7:85)*

4. *So she [Mary] veiled herself apart from them. Then We sent to her Our spirit, so he appeared to her in the image of a well-shaped human being. (19:17)*

5. *Next He rightly shaped him [Adam] and He breathed into him from His spirit, and He placed for you all hearing and eyes and hearts— how little thankful you all are! (32:9)*

6. *When your Lord said to the angels: "Verily I am creating a human-animal (bashar) from clay. So when I have rightly shaped him and I have breathed into him from My spirit, then you all bow down to him, prostrating yourselves." (38:71–72)*

7. *[God it is] Who raises up the stages, Possessor of the Throne: He casts the spirit from His Command upon whomever He wishes among His servants, that he might warn of the Day of the Encounter. (40:15)*

8. *And likewise We have inspired in you a spirit from Our Command . . . (42:52)*

9. *And He supported them with a spirit from Him . . . (58:22)*

Traditional Sayings

The following sayings are transmitted in the chapter on the Spirit from the *Uṣūl al-Kāfī:*[4]

1. Ahwal said: I asked Imam (Ja'far) Sādiq about the spirit that God breathed into Adam, according to His saying (Qur'an 15:29; 38:72): . . . *So when I have rightly shaped him and I have breathed into him from My spirit.* . . . He replied: "That spirit was created, and so was the spirit that was in Jesus."

2. Hamran said: I asked Imam Sādiq about God's saying [in regard to Jesus, at 4:171] *". . . and a spirit from Him . . . ."* He replied: "That is the created spirit of God: He created it in the body of Adam and in Jesus."

3. Muhammad ibn Muslim said: I asked Imam Sādiq about God's saying (at 15:29; 39:72) . . . *and I have breathed into him from My spirit* . . . : How did that "inbreathing" take place? He answered: "The spirit moves like the wind, and it is only called 'spirit' (*rūh*, in Arabic) because that expression is derived from (the Arabic root for) 'wind' (*rīh*): so the word 'spirit' was taken from the word for 'wind' because the spirits are similar to the wind. Now God connected that Spirit to Himself (in those Qur'anic passages) because He had specially chosen and selected it above all the other spirits. Likewise He called only one house—the Kaaba—'My' *House*,[5] only one of His messengers—Abraham—'My' *Intimate-friend*, and so on. So each (of those spirits) was created, formed, manifested, and sustained (by God)."

4. Muhammad ibn Muslim said: I asked Imam Bāqir about the widely reported saying *"God created Adam in His own image."* He replied: "That was a newly created form that God specially selected and chose above all the other different forms. So He connected that form and that spirit with Himself, as in His calling (the Kaaba) 'My' *House* and . . . *I have breathed into him from My spirit* . . . (15:29; 38:72)."

Now if we examine the meaning of the Qur'anic verses just cited and the substance of the above-mentioned sayings (of the Imams), we know that the "spirit," whose name (*rūh*) is derived from "wind" (*rīh*), is a creature like the air, created from the divine Breath. Or to put it simply, it is the life-giving flow of the Creator's supporting and sustaining Breath. Thus Adam's bodily form of clay only became alive when the breath of the spirit was breathed into it.

Now that it is clear, for intelligent readers, how the spirit was created, *one of the distinctive qualities of the spirit is that no body*

*can be alive and maintain itself (as a living being) without being
endowed with a spirit.*

Part Three: Establishing the Immortality of the Spirit

As for establishing the immortality of the spirit, many different philosophic arguments and scriptural attestations have been brought forward in the writings of the specialists on this subject. Since it would
take too long to mention all those arguments (in detail), we will give
a summary outline here, which should suffice to remove any doubt
for intelligent readers.

Rational Arguments

1. Given that the original Cause of causes and Everlasting Source (of
existence) is immortal and everlasting, it is self-evident that the effusion of the emanations of Its Light should also be eternal. For example,
the radiant particles of the light of the sun flow through and are reflected by all the things that exist (in the material world). As long as
the sun exists and continues to shine, the particles of its light will also
not cease to exist. Likewise the air surrounds and flows through all
things: certainly as long as the air exists, its effects will also continue
to exist. *Consequently those spirits—which have come into being
through God's Will and His Command, and which continue to exist
through the bountiful effusion of the overflowing emanation of Grace
of the Supreme Source and the inbreathing of His Power—are also
immortal.*

2. If we examine the bodily dimension of every being, (we observe) that from the beginning of its formation and the establishment
of its specific natural constitution on through until the end of its existence, every shape and form and figure is constantly undergoing
change and transformation. For example (the human being) passes
through the stages of *the extract* (of Clay), *the droplet, the clot, the embryo*
and the fetus; then from childhood and youth through old age and
death.[6] Yet at the same time, that original "self"—which is the underlying ground of its substance, quiddity, and essential identity—never
disappears from it. So indeed *this essential "self" is something other
than the body, its organic life, or any of the parts of the body.*

In other words, none of the different states of life and death have
any influence on or relevance to the actual significance of the expression "the self." For all of those things happen in relation to the (ongoing reality) of the "self." This (essential reality of the self) is what we

ordinarily refer to in the Persian language as *"I/my,"*[7] as in *"my* soul," *"my* body," *"my* limbs," *"my* life," *"my* death," and so on.

Thus, if we pay attention to the ultimate implications of these points, it is confirmed that *the spirit is something everlasting*, which does not disappear with the dissolution and annihilation of the body.

3. In those existents that have the power of thought and imagination, whether human beings or others, we often observe that while they are preoccupied with thinking about some particular matter, they forget the different parts of their body. But in no state do they ever become unaware of their "self."

4. There is an obvious difference between those incidents that affect each human being's *essence* (i.e., their "self" or spirit) and those that affect their body. This is evident in the case of an insane person with a healthy body, an intelligent person with a sick body, and so forth.

5. *Those qualities that describe the rational soul, such as knowing, understanding, perceiving, discerning, willing, and choosing*, cannot be attributed to any of the parts of the body. The body, with regard to its motions and states of rest and the like, can only be an *instrument* for carrying out the will of the rational soul (the spirit).

Scriptural References

The most decisive and categorical scriptural confirmations in this regard are verses of the Qur'an, including the following ones:

> 1. *Verily We created the human being (insān) from an extract of Clay. Next, We made him a droplet in a secure resting place. Next, We made the droplet into a blood clot, then We created the blood clot as an embryo, then We created the clot as bones, then We covered over the bones with flesh. Next, We brought him forth in another creation—so blessed be God, the Most-Beautiful/ Best of Creators! Next, after that, verily you all are dying. Next, on the Day of Resurrection, verily you all are being raised up!* (23:12–16)

The aim of these verses is to clearly specify that the creation of the *spirit* is different from that of the body. For it is only after mentioning the different stages of the bodily creation, from the *"extract (of Clay)"* to *"flesh,"* that God then goes on to mention the subsequent stages (of the *spirit's* development)—from *"next We brought him forth in another creation"* until the end of the verse.

2. *When God said to Jesus: "O Jesus, verily I am receiving you
and raising you up to Me . . ." (3:55)*

The meaning here is that what dies is the elemental, material
body, while what continues to survive and returns to God is precisely
the spirit.

3. *Don't ever consider those who have been killed in the way of
God to be dead! No, they are alive with their Lord, and He is
providing for them. (3:169)*

The meaning of this is that the body is what disappears, while
the spirit lives on eternally and enjoys all the blessings of the Creator's
Grace.

4. *And their saying: "Surely we killed the Messiah, Jesus the son
of Mary." But they did not kill him . . . certainly they did not kill
him! (4:157)*

The point here is that (Jesus's) opponents saw that his *body* was
killed, but the spirit most certainly will never be killed.

5. *And no one belongs to the people of the (divine) Book but the
one who most surely has faith in Him before his dying, and on
the Day of Resurrection there will be a witness against them!*
(4:159)

The meaning here is that a person's lack of faith before they die
will continue to affect their spirit, because it is always remaining (for
eternity). Otherwise it would not matter that there is a witness against
them at the Resurrection.

6. *And He is All-Powerful over His servants, and He sends
guardians over you all until, when death comes to one of you,
Our messengers receive that person, and they are not remiss (in
that task). Then they are returned to God, the Master of what is
their due: certainly the Judgment is His, and He is the Fastest of
Reckoners! (6:61–62)*

The point of these verses is that the body is what dies, while
what is brought back for the reckoning (at the Judgment) is the spirit.
What is referred to here as *"then they are returned to God, the Master of*

what is their due" is described in certain sayings (of the Prophet or Imams) as "the terror of the sudden vision (of death)."[8]

> 7. *Surely We created the human being (insān) from a mixed drop, that We may test him: then We made him hearing and seeing. (76:2)*

The meaning of this is that what is tested by imposing the responsibilities of the divine commandments and prohibitions is precisely that rational soul, which is described (in this verse) by the attribute of *"hearing and seeing"*—not the body or any of its parts.

Now for people of wisdom and spiritual insight, these rational arguments and attestations from religious tradition should be enough to establish the immortality of the spirit. May they be properly received by those who are deeply reflective.

"And God knows best the true reality of things."

Chapter Three

The Gathering, Reawakening, and Returning (of the Spirit) in the Realm of Return

Of course it is necessary, before we can enter into the heart of the matter, to be familiar with the meaning of these four (technical Arabic eschatological) expressions in order to facilitate the understanding of this subject at the appropriate points. Although each of these terms has a wide range of meanings, those meanings that are relevant to this particular subject are as follows:

- The *"Gathering"* (*hashr*) means to "collect" or to "bring together." In the technical language of the religious scholars,[1] it refers to the bringing together of the dead on the Day of the Rising, which they call "the Day of Gathering."

- The word *"Reawakening"* (*nashr*) means literally "scattering" or "spreading out." In the technical language of the religious scholars, (it refers to) the coming back to life and giving of life to the dead after the raising up of their bodies.

- The *"Returning"* (*mu'ād*) means coming back to the realm of Return.

- The realm of *Return* (*ma'ād*: 28:55) means literally "the place to which one comes back": in the technical language of the religious scholars, it refers to the Return (of the spirit) to the realm of *the other world*,[2] or to the spirits' return to their original, elemental, this-worldly bodies for the reckoning of their good and bad actions and the assignment of the corresponding rewards and punishments.

Now that the meanings of the basic terminology of this subject have been introduced, it is necessary to clarify the wider philosophic context of the immortality of the spirit and its Return. It is obvious that the subject of the Return will only be clarified once we have properly understood the following four fundamental principles:

1. Where does the existence of the different beings come from, and by what means (are they brought into existence)?

2. What are the specific effects or distinctive qualities that result from the bringing into existence of the different beings?

3. What duties are incumbent on each being, for as long as it exists, within the limits of its own capacity of understanding?

4. Where should (each being) be going? Or in other words, what is the ultimate goal of each being's destiny?

Now since each of these four fundamental principles can be investigated on the basis of the (classical Aristotelian) four causes—that is, the efficient, material, formal, and final causes—we will now explore the connections between those four causes and the wider philosophic context of each of these four fundamental principles.

The Perspectives (on These Metaphysical Questions)
Provided by the Four Causes

First, with respect to the *efficient*[3] cause: every existent thing—except for the existence of the Necessary Being—has not nor will not derive its existence from its own self, but rather as the effect of the causality of an efficient cause.

Second, with respect to the *material* cause: the bringing into existence of every thing is dependent on the appropriately receptive material substrate for that being. For example, the art of carpentry requires the material receptivity of wood, the material of cotton or wool is needed for spinning and weaving, and so on. The reason we speak of an "appropriately receptive" matter is that not every material, in itself, has the capacity to receive every sort of form: for example, not every rock can become a ruby or agate.

Third and fourth, with respect to the *formal* and *final* causes: Once the maker (the efficient cause) and the appropriately receptive material have been provided, a specific composite form (which is the formal cause) is brought into being to fulfill a specifically intended purpose—that intended purpose being what is called the "final cause." For example, a chair is constructed for sitting, a carpet is woven to be spread out (over the floor), cloth is manufactured for clothing, and so on.

The Philosophy Underlying the Four Fundamental Principles

1. All existent things come into existence from the void of nonexistence through the effusion of the overflowing emanation of the Grace of the Necessary Being, by the intermediary of their primary and secondary causes and effects. This is because the bringing into existence of those beings is a necessary consequence of the overflowing emanation of the Essence of the Necessary Being, just as the radiating of light is a necessary concomitant of the sun—but with this difference: that the overflowing emanation of the Essence of the Necessary Being is through His Will and freely bestowed Giving, while the shining of the sun is by nature and involuntary.

2. *The effect and distinctive quality resulting from the bringing into existence of the different ranks of beings is to demonstrate and manifest the eternal divine Essence and to make (the Essence) knowable so that (the beings) can reach the goal of Perfection.* For this is the ultimate goal of the overflowing emanation of His Grace, the Perfection that is sought through all the existent things: to be brought out of nonexistence into existence; to attain, through that existence, the final perfection of existence; and then, after having reached the perfection of existence, to be reunited with the Necessary Being.

That is exactly what was intended by His saying:[4] "*I was a hidden Treasure, and I loved that I should be known; so I created creation/the creatures*[5] *so that I might be known.*" Apart from this (primordial creative Love), God is without any sort of needfulness in any respect; He does not need to create the creatures so that He might be known.

3. *The duty of every being, for as long as it exists, is this: to strive and go to every length to pass through the stages of the process of its gradual perfection, to the extent that its power of understanding and its bodily strength allow—without anguish, unnecessary difficulty,*[6] *or unbearably painful impositions.*

This is as it says in the Qur'an: *God does not impose* (as a responsibility) *upon any soul except what it is* (within) *its capacity* (2:286); and:
*And there is nothing for the human being but what he strives for—and what
he was striving for shall surely be seen!* (53:39–40).

4. *Where* should (each being) be going? In fact, in order to understand this subject properly, we first need to know where each being
has come *from*, so that we can come to know where it ought to be
headed. In other words, we first need to perceive what the Source[7] (of
existence) really is, so that we can see clearly what the "Return" (to
that Source) is.

[Coming to Know Being and the Changes in Its Substance
through the Process of Spiritual Perfection][8]

Hence the proper understanding of the nature of the Source depends
on our coming to know *"Being"*[9] and the transformations of its substance in the course of the process of perfection of its essential nature.
This (universal process of spiritual perfection, or of the ongoing transformation of Being) can be presented in summary form as follows:

[The "Origination" of the spirit (*mabda'*):] Each thing that exists
comes into existence only once the necessary conditions for its existence have been brought together for it. Then at that initial moment,
the originating principle for bringing into existence the substance of
each thing is this: that by the active Will of the Necessary Being, it
passes from the void of nothingness and—having traversed the stage
of possible being between existence and nonexistence—sets foot in the
realm of actual existence, so that it can now be called an existent thing.
Now that "thing-hood" (of each existent being) is called "the *spirit*,"
in the technical terminology used by people of the different religions:
that is, something that is subtle and transcends matter and form.[10]

[The spirit's "Return" (*ma'ād*):] However, **the final point of the
process of perfection of every creature is when it becomes the perfectly
pure alloy, through integrating within itself the distinctive qualities
of all the influences of the different natures of (all) the creatures, from
the Source of the highest world on down to the bottom of the lowest
world.** So it is evident that the creature who reaches that condition
attains the Truth and the True Reality, finds Perfection through reunion with God, and returns to the eternal abode of the Return.

As it says in the Qur'an: *They said: "Verily we are God's, and to
Him we are surely returning!"* (2:156). And it also says: *Every soul is
tasting death. Then to Us you all are being returned!* (29:57). And it says
as well: *God begins the creation. Then He repeats it again. Then to Him you*

all are returned! (30:11). And there are a great many more verses in the Qur'an reiterating this same meaning.[11]

Based on the conditions outlined above, every creature after its initial appearance (in existence), in order to complete its process of perfection, must move from its original station (with its Creator)[12] in the arc of ascent into the arc of descent (of actual manifestation),[13] since every movement from a higher to a lower position necessarily involves a descending course. After that initial descending movement, it then begins its own arc of spiritual ascent, thereby completing its circular movement (of return to its divine Source)—since otherwise the spirit's existence would remain incomplete and fruitless. It would be like our drawing a circle using a compass: if all the points of the circumference were not completed by means of the rotating movement (of the compass arm) around the center point, then that circle would remain incomplete.

As for why (each creature) starts to move at the very beginning down the arc of descent, that is because the primary cause of its initial existentiating movement from the ultimate Source is the Will of the Necessary Being. Thus (each new creature) must necessarily pass through all the stages of cause and effect, from its relative immateriality,[14] by means of its initial (subtle) materiality,[15] through the combinations of elemental matter and form, until it reaches the lowest stages of the (creational) arc of descent.

At that point, thanks to the "provisions" that it has accumulated as a result of the influences acquired during its initial descending movement, (the spirit) begins to pursue the ascending stages of its upward movement along the path of spiritual perfection through the higher realms of existence. Thus it passes step by step through the (ascending) spiritual stages of the *Kingdom*,[16] *Rulership*,[17] Dominion, God-ness, and Essence,[18] until it reaches its final Perfection.[19]

(The necessity for this gradual ascending movement of the spirit's perfection) can be compared to the fact that although an essential part of the human state is the potential *capacity* for literacy, a person cannot become truly literate until they have passed in succession through each class in the ascending stages of instruction, beginning with primary school and finishing with the cycles of higher education. Thus it is only at that culminating station (of the process of spiritual perfection) that we can truly understand what are the real experiential qualities of the Gathering, the Reawakening, and the eternal Return, or what actually constitutes the rewards and recompenses (for good deeds) and the punishments for sins. *The Knowledge* (of that) *is with God!* (67:26).

Now that we have clarified the underlying philosophy of the Return and to whom it applies, we can start by leaving out of the remaining discussion those individuals who have absolutely no belief in the existence of any sort of Return. That would include the pure materialists[20] and any others who maintain that "when you die, it's all over." So to continue with our essential goal (in this discussion):

The Return (*ma'ād*), which is the ultimate spiritual station and the final place of return for those (spirits) who are being "gathered up" and "reawakened" in the realm of the other world, has been described and depicted in many different ways. In other words, those who believe in the Return form a variety of different groups, including the following ones:

- First group: those who believe in a *purely bodily* Return;

- Second group: those who believe in a *purely spiritual* Return;

- Third group: those who believe in the *harmonization* (combination) of *both* a bodily and spiritual Return;

- Fourth group: the proponents of *the process of spiritual perfection* (*sayr-i takāmul*);

- Fifth group: the proponents of *tanāsukh* (the purely earthly transmigration of all souls, in all directions). They include several branches, each of which will be treated in its appropriate place (in chapter 8), God willing.

- There is also a sixth group of those who hesitate between some of the above views:[61] that is, those who believe in the Return, but who don't express any definite and certain idea, and who are unsure as to which of the above-mentioned groups has the correct and sound beliefs.

In any case, since the statements of those who are uncertain about the matter of the Return don't give any decisive result, they can be excluded from the subject of the following discussions, which will include the basis for the beliefs of each of the first five above-mentioned groups.

Chapter Four

The Purely Bodily Return

This is the belief held by most of the theologians, jurists, and official leaders of the religions of the "people of the (revealed) Book," including the books of the Torah, Gospels, Qur'an, and others. Moreover, the majority of Muslims, in addition to the literal text of the verses of the Qur'an, have also taken into consideration the transmitted reports of the hadith (of the Prophet) and traditions of the holy Imams.

The proponents of this view say that since the Return of the bodies (of the dead at the Last Day) is something that the religious experts among the people of the Book have accepted and come to agree upon by consensus, as is required by the literal texts of (God's) Word in the divine Scriptures and the widely transmitted reports (of the teachings of the Prophet and Imams), they consider the belief in the bodily Return to be one of the essential elements of religion; so they consider whoever denies that to be an opponent (of the true religion). In particular, (this group maintains that) the verses of the Qur'an concerning the Return are so unambiguously clear that they don't allow any room for interpretation. Since that is the case, the reasonings of an (opposing) group of philosophers—based on things like "the impossibility of bringing back what was annihilated," the objection concerning "the beast of prey and the person who is eaten,"[1] and the claim that the impossibility of this (material bodily Return) is "self-evident," and the like[2]—are all groundless and absolutely without foundation. On the contrary, given the absolute Power of the

Creator to bring (any) creature into being, there is nothing to prevent (God's) bringing back what was annihilated, or overcoming the objections about the predator and the person who is eaten and the like.

Moreover, [these theologians continue] that original *"Clay,"*[3] the essential substance and "self" of the being that was brought from nonexistence into existence in the first place, is the real basis for what we are considering here. And that (essential substance), because of the survival of the spirit, is not annihilated by the destruction and annihilation of the (dead) body, so that the whole problem of the "impossibility of bringing back what was annihilated" doesn't even enter into this discussion. For just as that (essential substance) was nonexistent to begin with and then came into existence through the Will of the Almighty and took on the shape of a material, corporeal body, so likewise through God's Will it will again come to exist in a living, corporeal form, as a body endowed with a spirit. This is just like what is reported in (the following report recorded in) the *Kāfī*:[4]

> Imam Ja'far al-Sādiq was asked: "Does the dead body disintegrate?" He replied: "Yes, insofar as neither its flesh nor its bones remain—only that Clay (or essential substance: *tīnat*) from which it was created. For that does not disintegrate, and it will remain in the grave in a (potentially) 'recurrent' form until God creates that person from it once again, just as He created him the first time."

Besides, all the great prophets were basically in agreement in what they said about this matter—that is, about the *bodily* Gathering, Reawakening, and Return. So no one could possibly have faith in those prophets and at the same time deny the bodily Gathering and Reawakening; those two things cannot be combined.

Now the arguments and proofs brought forward by the proponents of the bodily Return are quite numerous, but they are also so very well known that there is no need to mention them all here. If it is necessary, one can consult the (theological) books relating to this subject. Here it should be sufficient to refer to the considerable number of Qur'anic verses—288 in all—which the late Majlisī mentioned in support of this claim, in his (famous compendium of Shiite tradition) *Bihār al-Anwār*.[5]

In connection with this, it should be mentioned that the believers in the Return of the body also fall into two groups:

The First Group [who argue for the Return of a newly recreated material "likeness" of the original body, but without the very same elemental constituents] say: "God Almighty annihilates the parts (of the dead body) of the creature, then He causes them to return."[6] The gist of this is that after the dissolution of the (bodily) parts of the creature, God once again—through His absolute Power—newly brings back into existence an exact *likeness* (of the original body) in every respect, but not with the same (elemental parts).

In support of this they cite various Qur'anic verses, including the following ones:

- *To Him is your place of returning, all of you together—the Promise of God is True! Surely God begins the creation, then He brings it back . . . , and also Say: "God begins the creation, then after that He brings it back." (10:4, 34)*

- *Then they will be saying: "Who will bring us back?" Say: "The One Who created you all the first time. . . ." (17:51)*

- *From it We created you all, and in it We are returning you all, and out of it We are bringing you all yet another time. (20:55)*

- *On the Day We roll up the sky as a scroll is rolled up for the writings: just as We began the first creation, We are bringing it back—a promise* (incumbent) *on Us, for surely We are doing* (that)! (21:104)

- *Does not He Who begins the creation, then He brings it back . . . ? (27:64)*

- *Or do they not see how God begins the creation, then He brings it back? Surely that is easy for God! (29:19)*

- *God begins the creation, then He brings it back, then to Him you all are returned. (30:11)*

- *And He is the One Who begins the creation; then He brings it back, and that is simpler for Him. . . . (30:27)*

- *Verily He it is Who begins and brings back. (85:13)*

The Second Group [who argue for the literal Return of "exactly the same" material body] say: "God Most-High causes the creatures to die and disperses their parts; then He rejoins (the parts) and returns life to them."[7] The gist of this is that God causes the creatures to die, and the parts (of their bodies) are then separated and scattered. Then He brings those scattered parts back together just as they were, with the same quantities and qualities as before—*exactly the same parts*—and gives them back their life, in the same original shape and form they had during their first lifetime. (According to this group), since God has the Power to create the first creation and all the movements and transformations of the cycle of life—from the initial "droplet" and the embryo through adolescence, adulthood, old age, death, and the resurrection—so likewise He is also Capable of bringing together all the scattered parts and particular aspects of that (original human body).

As an argument for supporting their own belief, this second group likewise cite various Qur'anic verses, including the following:

- *And when Abraham said: "O my Lord, show me how You give life back to the dead." He said: "Or did you not have faith?" He replied: "Yes indeed! Yet so that my heart might be at peace." He said: "So take four birds and cut them apart for yourself, then place a part of them on each mountain. Then call to them—they will come to you running. And know that God is Most Glorious, All-Wise!"* (2:260)

- *So how* (will it be), *when We have brought them together on a Day of which there is no doubt . . . ?* (3:25)

- *God, there is no god but He. He is certainly gathering you all together to the Day of the Rising, of which there is no doubt. Who is more sincere in speaking than God?!* (4:87)

- *Say: "To whom is all that is in the heavens and the earth?" Say: "To God!" He imposed for Himself Loving-kindness: He certainly brings you all together for the Day of the Rising—there is no doubt about it! Those who have damaged their selves/souls, they have no faith.* (6:12)

- *And We left some of them, on that Day, making waves in others. Then it is blown into the Horn/forms[8]—and lo, We have brought them all together!* (18:99)

- *Say: "God brings you all to life; then He causes you all to die; then He brings you all together for the Day of the Rising—there is no doubt of that." And yet most of the people do not know!* (45:26)

Chapter Five

The Purely Spiritual Return

Now this is the belief of the majority of the sages among the philosophers and followers of the Peripatetic[1] school, who have explored and carefully investigated this matter, based on their analysis and rational and symbolic interpretation of the religious scriptures and their philosophy concerning the spiritual realities. In summary, they say: After the separation of the spirit from the body (at death) and the disintegration of the material body, what is able to survive and continue will be precisely that spirit, or the rational soul.

In other words, what never disappears, under any condition or circumstance, is precisely that original, substantial "essential reality" (that is) the existential core of its very being, the essence of its "self," and the underlying being of its existence. For after the breaking of the relationship between the self and body (at death) and the dissolution and disintegration of the bodily corpse, it is self-evident that the body becomes obliterated and nonexistent. So it can't be brought back and return in its previous state, since according to the fundamental principles of science and the laws of reason, bringing back (into existence) what has been annihilated is both logically and really impossible.

The evidence for this is that *God is absolutely All-Powerful and Capable of (creating) every thing, but He never attaches His Will to anything that is really or logically impossible.* Therefore, according to the necessary law of nature—and that nature is precisely what the absolutely All-Powerful (Creator) has brought into

73

existence on the foundation of Wisdom and Justice, in order to maintain all the intrinsic orders of the creatures—*the (divinely established) course*[2] *of each thing cannot be changed.* So only the spirit can survive and be eternal.

As it was stated by a philosopher quoted by the late (Shiite theologian) Majlisī in his book *Bihār al-Anwār:*[3] "The philosophers and the theologians are in agreement about the real existence of the Return, but they disagree as to how it actually takes place. Most of the philosophers maintain that the Return is purely spiritual, because they say that both the forms and the accidental (elements) of the body are annihilated (after death) and cannot be returned. But the soul is an immaterial[4] substance that is immortal and cannot disappear; so after the cutting of its connections (with the body), it returns to the world of immaterial beings." And in the Qur'an it says: . . . *They said: "Surely we are God's, and to Him we are returning!"* (156:2).

Therefore, in light of what has already been established concerning the immortality of the spirit,[5] it is certain that the rewards and punishments, recompenses and penalties of each person's good and bad actions correspond to the *dimensions/perceptions of the other world*[6] in the following way: "the spirits of the blessed and those who do good" are eternally rejoicing and filled with joy through their perception of the sensations (*nash'a*) of the pleasures of the perfections they acquired in this world, in the form in which they had represented them in their thoughts. Such a state has been interpreted as (corresponding to) the eternal paradise.[7]

(Likewise) "the spirits of the criminals and wrongdoers" are eternally tormented, shamed, and pained by the perception of the sensations of the pains (due to their) ignorance and the lowly, blameworthy attributes they acquired in this world. Such a state resembles that eternal place of suffering of which it says in the Qur'an: *Verily, whoever is brought to his Lord as a wrongdoer, Gehenna is for him: there he is neither dying nor living!* (20:74). And it also says: *The one who is burning in the Greatest Fire: then he is neither dying there nor is he living!* (3:12–13).

Of course there are (many other) Qur'anic verses pointing to the "dimensions/sensations (*nasha'āt*) of the other world," including the following ones:

> *Say: "Travel through the earth, then consider how He began the creation." Next God brought forth the dimension (nash'a) of the other world: truly God is Capable of every thing!* (29:20)

As well as:

*And that the other dimension/bringing-forth (al-nash'at al-ukhrā)
is* (incumbent) *upon Him.* (53:47)

And also:

*Now surely you all have already known the first dimension/bring-
ing-forth (al-nash'at al-ūlā), so why do you not reflect/recollect?!*
(56:62)

Now it is essential to understand that this dimension (*nash'a*) we
are investigating has two aspects:

The First Aspect: "the *General* Spiritual Dimension/Sensation
(of all beings)":

This (universal, vital spiritual) dimension[8] is the same for *all* of
the creatures existing both in this world and in the other world. In
other words, their different positions in the chain of being, their differing levels, and the qualitative and quantitative (differences) specific
to each creature do not affect this dimension in any way at all. (This
universal spiritual dimension includes) such things as the life-giving
influx, the transubstantial movement underlying the process of perfection, self-awareness, the instinct of self-preservation, the faculties of
anger and desire, the instinct for repelling what is harmful and acquir-
ing what is beneficial, the sensations of pleasure and pain, the experience of dying and of the spirit's separating from the body and entering
the other world, and so on. This single dimension/vital sensation
applies to all of (the creatures), because every existent thing was first
nonexistent and then was created by the Will of the Creator of everything; and because every existent thing has a beginning and a goal,
and is subject to the (same) fundamental principles of creation and
existence, to the essential requirements of their spiritual and bodily
natures in all these areas. That is why it says in the Qur'an: . . . *Each
group is rejoicing in what is with them.* (23:53; 30:32).

The Second Aspect: the "*individual* spiritual sensations":[9]

The number of these (individual, personal) sensations corresponds
to the number of individual existent beings. For the impact of the
sensations of the other world will appear differently in every being,
depending on the (distinctive) qualities and quantities and the specific
individual perceptions unique to that particular being.

This is why, with regard to the planet Earth, there are verses of
the Qur'an not only concerning the "Gathering" (in the other world)

of humans, but also alluding to the "Gathering" of the animals as well as all the other beings, and to their returning as well in the realm of the Return. Those verses include His saying:

> *There is no animal crawling on the earth, nor any bird flying with its two wings, but that they are communities like you all. We have not neglected in the Book any thing. Then to their Lord/ Sustainer they all are being gathered up.* (6:38)

Also:

> *And on the Day We cause the mountains to move, and you see the earth standing out, and We have gathered them up—for We have not left one of them behind!* (18:47)

And also:

> *And when the mountains are made to move, and when the pregnant camels are set loose, and when the wild animals are gathered up. . . .* (81:3–5)

Given all this, as far as the people of faith who believe in the Gathering are concerned, there are simply no grounds for denial or hesitation.

In connection with this topic, we should also take into account that it has frequently happened that when living human individuals (on earth) come into contact with the spirits of those who have died, whether in dreams or under other circumstances, they have perceived that (newly imparted) information about the dimensions/perceptions of the other world as having the same distinctive qualities as their own ordinary, habitual mental experiences. That is not improbable, since as was already suggested earlier, the spirits themselves (in the other world) also perceive those (other-worldly) perceptions/dimensions, both of pleasures and of pains, according to the forms in which they have represented them in their own thoughts. *For the other world is like a mirror: everyone sees their own form in it.*

This has been a summary of the beliefs of those who believe in the purely spiritual Return. Of course in addition to all the supporting evidence already mentioned, this group also has many other arguments in favor of their claims, based on rational premises and on traditional sources. There is no need to mention all of those arguments here, given the possibility (for our readers) of referring to the relevant books of wisdom and philosophy, since doing so would unnecessarily lengthen this discussion.

In conclusion, there is one more point we should mention, which is that even the proponents of a bodily Return do not necessarily reject the spiritual Return outright, as the careful scholar Ravānī suggested in his book *Sharh al-'Aqā'id*[10] and as the late Majlisī also wrote in his book *Bihār al-Anwār*:[11] "And know that the bodily Return is something in whose existence (the person of true faith) must believe; whoever denies that should be considered an opponent of the faith. There is no religious obligation to believe in the spiritual Return, which is the soul's taking pleasure and suffering from incorporeal pleasures and pains after its separation from the body; so the person who denies that should not be considered an opponent of the faith. Nor is there anything in reason or religious tradition that would prevent the affirmation of that (spiritual Return)."

Chapter Six

The Harmonization of a Bodily and Spiritual Return

Those who maintain this belief (in the harmonious combination of a bodily and spiritual Return) are a group of dedicated seekers of the truth[1] from every community, including scholars, sages, philosophers, and others. Each one of them, in their own writings, have stated the essentials of what needed to be said. They have explained this by means of clear arguments and decisive proofs, based on both scriptural and rational grounds, by means of responses that refute (all possible opposition) and resolve (any difficulties), all of which they have recorded in their writings. And they have done so to such an extent that there is no room left for their opponents to bring up any further argument or investigation.

In other words, they have so well explained and resolved and distinguished the ways in which the bodily and spiritual Returns are harmonized and combined that they have left no ground for their opponents to stand on. So that even if those who might wish to contradict them should try to do so, out of ignorance or fanaticism, such (attempts) are to be considered groundless and mere rhetorical flourishes.[2] For through a process of objective comparison, they have managed to coordinate and bring into harmony with each other all of the (relevant and solid) arguments of the proponents of *both* the physical and the spiritual Return, by taking into account the rules of logic, scriptural indications, rational conceptions, and philosophic proofs and arguments. In doing so they have removed every possible source of objection. Their thoroughgoing approach confirms (the proverbial saying): "When you get to 100, you also have 90."

Among other things, what they say is this:[3] Since it was established and made known in the discussion concerning the immortality of the spirit[4] that the survival of the spirit (after bodily death) and the life of the (earthly) body are two different things, then by the same token it must be acknowledged that the perceptions (*nash'a*) of pleasures and pains of each of them (i.e., of the spirit in the other world, and of the body in this world) are also different from each other. Now the spirit is a being that is subtle in nature and connected with the immaterial beings (*mujarradāt*) of the Highest world, while the elemental body is gross and heavy and tied to the lowest world. In other words, the spirit will always have an inclination toward the ascending movement through the worlds of the (divine) *Kingship*, Dominion,[5] and the higher realms, as a consequence of its essential immateriality. While the body, given the natural requirements of its elemental, this-worldly nature, will always incline, by a descending movement, toward this dense world of earthly matter.[6]

That is why *the body, because of its connection with material life, will not be able to perceive the sensations (nasha'āt) of the spiritual realm as long as it is under the influence of the desires and passions of the domineering self.*[7] As for the spirit, or rational soul, because of its subtle (immaterial) substance, it will never be concerned with the sensations of this material world, which are below its state.

From another perspective, according to rational logic and scientific principles, every beginning has an ultimate end, every start has a finish, everything that originates has its place of return, and every first has its last—except for the Essence of the Creator, Which always was, is, and will be. Hence the process of the Return is real, right, and necessary;[8] and all of the beings must be "gathered up" at a definite time and according to a specific order.

Thus God, through His perfect Power and all-encompassing Wisdom, will gather up (all the creatures) on the Day of the Raising-up, which is the Day of the Resurrection and the "Greater Rising." (He will do so) by means of removing the opposition between the intrinsic requirements of matter and the source of life of the spirit and body, and by combining, joining, and mixing the body and spirit in some qualitatively and quantitatively special way—whether that be by gathering together the dispersed bodily parts, by bringing back (the former body), or in some other way. It is obvious that such a distinctive *composite* dimension of being (*nash'a*) would be quite different from those perceptions/dimensions that the proponents of a purely bodily or a purely spiritual Return had conceived.

Given what has been said here—and with further reference to the detailed exposition of the statements of the proponents of a harmonized, combined bodily and spiritual Return in their books on that subject—it is certain that whenever this matter is judged on the basis of fairness and true impartiality, there will no longer be any room for disagreement between any of the above-mentioned groups concerning the harmonization of those two sorts of Return.

"And God knows best what is correct."

Chapter Seven

The (Spirit's) Return by Way of the Process of Perfection

General Principles

Those who believe in the Return by way of the process of perfection are in general those people who say: "Now it is self-evident that God, the Creator of all the creatures, has not created and does not create any creature without a purpose, since He is absolutely Wise and All-Knowing. Therefore when He brought into existence all the different created beings by means of their ultimate and immediate causes and effects, He established by nature a beginning and a goal for every being in every case, in accordance with His all-encompassing Wisdom. For only God is absolutely without any beginning or end. Otherwise, everything God has created is without exception subject to this rule: they must all reach their ultimate goal by passing through the stages between the two points of their beginning and their end. Therefore in everything that concerns Religion[1] as well, the ultimate goal of every being is to pass through certain specific stages between its coming into existence and its place of Return (to God) so that it can attain the Goal of its Returning in the other world, in the eternal realm of the Return."

Now the expression "the Return" (ma'ād), which means "the place of Returning" in Persian, has two different meanings.

1. The first is the exoteric, technical sense that has already been mentioned in the preceding chapters on the bodily, spiritual, and harmonized (both bodily and spiritual) notions of the Return.

2. The second meaning is that of the actual process of perfection: that is to say, (the spirit's) passing through various stages in order to reach its final goal, which is the stage of Perfection, the ultimate spiritual station of reunion with God, the Truly Real. This is attested to in the verse: *They said: "We are from God, and surely to Him we are returning."* (2:156)

So according to the proponents of the process of perfection, when the spirit leaves the body (at death), it does not return to that initial, material body, except for a few exceptional cases.[2] Indeed even among those who believe in a purely bodily Return—whether through the reuniting of the body's parts or the restoration of (another similar) body—the majority still hold that this takes place through the establishment of a new, composite body resembling the preceding body or through the likeness of an "imaginal form" that is embodied and raised up through the influence of the surviving spirit—not through the original material body that has died and disappeared.

In any case, we must also take into account the following point. Just as the various things that exist are all different with respect to their essential created dispositions, so they also differ among themselves with respect to their process of perfection: each particular group of existent creatures is given its own particular beginning and ultimate end in a way that is specific to that particular group. Now among groups of creatures are the beings on this planet, who are the subject of this book. Their own specific process of perfection is subject to certain conditions, in the following manner. Every existent thing that comes into being out of nothingness through the emanation of the overflowing Grace of the Necessary Being must necessarily become established, as a result of the vertical (creative) process of emanation,[3] at its own initial point of emergence in existence that has been determined to be appropriate for it. Then it begins its own process of perfection starting from that point.

However, those who have reflected on this matter are of two different opinions regarding the place and stage of existence where each (creature) is initially established after emerging from the process of emanation:

1. The first point of view is that since the process of bringing the existent things into being involves differing factors of cause-and-effect and temporal and spatial priority and posteriority, this necessarily gives rise, at the initial stage of their existence, to different degrees of distance or closeness to the Source, and to a greater or lesser intensity of their initial individual potential. However these (differences due to the particular) causes and effects do not involve any unjust discrimination, but rather conceal an aspect of divine Wisdom with regard to the ordering and arrangement of the specific characteristics of each nature for certain beneficial purposes. In addition, since the final goal of Perfection is ultimately the same for all the beings, their (initial) differences of priority or posteriority in the process of perfection will not have any (unfair) influence. In this view, every being that comes into existence initially at the (particular) stage of existence (determined for it), whether that be high or low, starts its process of perfection from that particular point. For example, if one being is a human-animal (*bashar*) in its initial existence while another being begins as a mineral, each one starts its process of perfection from its own particular initial stage of existence until it reaches its ultimate Goal, which is the same for all alike.

2. **The second point of view** is as follows: To begin with, as a consequence of God's absolute Justice, there must not be any (unfair) difference in the process of emanation of all the beings (from their Source), whatever the course of that process. Moreover, the natural movement of every thing is either from higher to lower or from lower to higher. Therefore, since for all beings the movements of their process of emanation have begun first of all with the Highest Source, they must necessarily follow that descending course (of existentiation) until they eventually reach the lowest point of their descending movement, which is the place of their emergence in existence. Then they begin their ascending process of perfection, (moving) from the lowest state to the highest.

Thus the factors of primary and intermediate causality and of relative priority and posteriority in time and place (cited by the proponents of the first point of view above) will have absolutely no effect on (each being's) initial point of emergence in existence. For even though every thing caused is *temporally* posterior to its primary cause, this temporal posteriority does not always have a determining effect on its distance or closeness to the Source, or on the intensity of its individual potentiality. Indeed there are all sorts of effects that are closer (to God) and more intense in their being than their own causes. For example, a ruby or another gemstone comes from an ordinary rock; a tree abounding in fruit comes from a seed-pit or tiny sapling; from an egg there comes a swift-winged bird; a single drop of semen gives rise to an animal or a human-animal (*bashar*); and sometimes there comes into being from an ordinary human-animal a genius or a prophet, and so on.

Furthermore, God is Just and His Grace is all-encompassing. So in particular, *all of the creatures are on the same equal footing with respect to their nature, their creation, and their direct relationship with the Creator, not at different levels.*

In any event, without even evaluating the relative merits of each of these two points of view, in general all the different levels of beings, whether higher or lower, must pursue their own particular process of perfection with the means that have been placed at their disposal. So eventually, having reached their highest possible stage, each of them will attain the final result corresponding to what they have come to merit through their own actions.

As for what was just mentioned about "higher" and "lower" (levels of existence), that must be understood to refer to the lower and higher levels of the initial process of emanation, and *only* from the point of view of the Creator, not the other creatures. Otherwise, as a consequence of the Justice of divine Providence, *the course of the process of perfection and its ultimate Goal are the same for every creature.*

For things have been established in such a way that even those beings that begin at the lowest level gradually advance and reach higher levels through the influence of transformations, changes, and metamorphoses that may happen internally and in a gradually ongoing movement, or through an external, discontinuous transfer, as with the ascension from minerals to plants, then to animals and higher states.[4] In other words, as long as (the creatures) have not acquired the ability to discern and discriminate between good and bad actions and have therefore not become responsible for their actions, they continue to ascend gradually through an automatic, orderly natural process of change, in accordance with unchangeable divine determinations that have been established in the essential nature of each being. However, from then on (after the creatures have acquired the power of moral discernment and responsibility), it is their actions that go on to determine their individual destinies. As the poet Hafez—may God's Mercy be with him—said:

> *How beautifully spoke the ancient peasant to his son:*
>
> *"O light of my eyes, you reap nothing but what you've sown!"*[5]

Thus the basic levels of beings, from lowest to highest, are in the following order:

1. Those beings that are "without sensation": these are the ones that, after they are destroyed, decompose (into their constituent material elements), while their vital influence appears in another thing at the same or a higher level, until they are gradually transformed into beings having sensation, and eventually into those with a spirit.

2. Beings possessing a "spirit without (moral) discernment": these have their own spirit that survives after their body passes away; their spirit moves up to higher stages (of being) through a gradual, natural process of ascension.

3. Beings possessing a "(morally) discerning spirit": those having the ability to distinguish between the good or evil of their own actions; they are therefore morally responsible for carrying out their various duties.

The movement of progressing toward perfection in those beings, once they have reached that point (of moral responsibility), takes place in the following manner. Every being possessing a discerning spirit[6] must, beginning with the particular body and material form in which it exists, pass through the different ascending stages of the process of perfection—a process that is both bodily and spiritual at the same time—in order to reach the final stage of perfection of body and spirit. In other words, just as we can visibly see and sense in the case of the physical bodies that each body, if no obstacle intervenes, will gradually pass from the initial existence of its living seed through its stages of development until it reaches its final stage of physical maturity: so likewise the spirit will become strengthened in its process of perfection, in a way corresponding to the gradual unfolding of its bodily powers, until it reaches the full perfection of its own intrinsic spiritual capacity. According to this law, then, it is necessary for the body and spirit of every single existent creature endowed with a spirit on the planet earth to pass through these spiritual stages through mutual cooperation.

It is self-evident that once these beings have attained their perfection, then their body will disappear and their spirit—after carrying out certain preparatory procedures and having passed through the process of accounting for all its actions—will be dispatched to its eternal abode, where it will everlastingly experience the ultimate outcome of its good and bad deeds. Of course what is actually meant by the expression "everlasting" here, or in whatever context that word may be used—as in referring to "eternal" rewards or penalties in the gardens of paradise, or hellfire, or the like—is only a relative sort of eternity. That is to say, those states will be "everlasting" as long as God so wills or as long as the created things remain in existence. For otherwise, as has already repeatedly been stated, only God's Essence— which was from all eternity and will be for all eternity—is *absolutely* Eternal, and nothing else: this is supported by the following verses of the Qur'an, among others:[7]

> *As for those who are distressed, they are in the Fire: there they have anguished moaning and bitter longing. Abiding there eternally, so long as the heavens and the earth endure, except for whatever your Lord may wish: certainly your Lord accomplishes whatever He wills! And as for those who have been blessed, they are in the Garden, abiding there eternally, so long as the heavens and the earth endure, except for whatever your Lord may wish— as a gift never cut off.* (11:106–108).

As well as:

> *... There is no god* (no object of worship) *but He: every thing is perishing except for His Face* (His Essence). *....* (28:88)

And also:

> *Every thing upon it* (the earth) *is passing away: there only remains the Face* (the Essence) *of your Lord, the Master of Majesty* (Greatness) *and Beneficence* (Generosity)*!* (55:26–27)

To conclude, those were the general principles underlying the subjects discussed by the proponents of the Return understood as the process of spiritual perfection.

[How the Return takes place, according to (the proponents of) the process of spiritual perfection, including four modalities:][8]

Now with regard to the particulars (of this group's understanding), although they all share a faith in the immortality of the spirit and in the reality of its Return, they have different ways of understanding how that Return actually takes place. Those different ways can be summed up in the following topics, which we will explain in the subsequent discussions:

> **First modality**: the process of perfection through "transposition" from the material world into the intermediate (spiritual) world.[9]

Second modality: the process of perfection through a "connection" between the intermediate world and the material world.

Third modality: the process of perfection through "accumulation" (of vital influences from the different lower levels) by means of the arc of ascent (through the mineral, plant, and animal realms).

Fourth modality: the "unitive" process of perfection, by means of the two combined arcs of ascent and descent.

First Modality—the Process of Perfection by "Transposition"
From the Material World to the Intermediate (Spiritual) World

As was already mentioned in the preceding discussion of general principles, in the case of each being endowed with a (morally) discerning spirit that succeeds in completing the process of perfection while in its initial body and material form, after death its spirit will be taken to its eternal abode and there will forever enjoy the fruits of its actions. However, if any sort of event or cause—such as the influence of its environment, or the reactions resulting from its (wrong) actions, or any other hindrance—should compel its ascending process of spiritual and/or bodily perfection to come to a stop, then at the time of separation from its material body, the spirit will be transferred and introduced, either immediately or after a delay,[10] directly into the intermediate world. So it is in *that* world that the necessary means for making up for those past problems will be put at the spirit's disposition, whatever the level at which its process of perfection was interrupted.

Now although God Almighty is Just and Equitable and judges every being with justice and equity, at the same time, because of His aspect of Mercy, Compassion, Loving-kindness, Generosity, and Beneficence, He also shows clemency to a certain extent toward those who have egregiously sinned or who have been heedless or have gone astray. Thus He brought into being the intermediate world (*barzakh*), which has also been called the "imaginal" world,[11] as an opportunity for those who had stopped in their process of perfection to make up for (their past errors), and so that His "*Proof*"[12] might be completed in every possible respect.

There, in that imaginal world, a (new) set of surroundings are transposed for each spirit that had stopped (in its earthly process of perfection), a milieu resembling its earthly, material surroundings during its earthly life—or, if necessary, a milieu that is more helpful. This takes place through the projection of sensations that are "transposed" from a material to a spiritual form of embodiment. There all the necessary means for the spirit that had stopped advancing in its (earthly) process of perfection are prepared and arranged in order to overcome its shortcomings, along with a sufficient period of time and in a way that greatly facilitates its task, without the obstacles and hindrances (of earthly life). So if that spirit takes full advantage of this special opportunity and favor (from God), it will be saved.[13] For once the period of the delay that has been established (for that spirit) has expired and it has finished clearing up its (spiritual) account, it will be brought to its eternal abode in the realm of the Return in the other world in order to receive the judgment and appropriate recompense for its actions.

Now since the intermediate world has just been mentioned, this is perhaps the right occasion to explain something of the distinctive features of that intermediate world in order to illuminate the minds of those who would like to understand it.

THE INTERMEDIATE WORLD (*Barzakh*)

The *barzakh* is a world situated between this material world and the realm of eternity, a world which is devoid of (this world's) spatial dimensions and temporality. In other words, the intermediate world is so unlimited with respect to its spatial capacity that, for example, all of the beings in creation, from the first to the last, could be brought together in that realm without ever restricting its capacity and relative extent in any way. This is just like the way it happens with all the thoughts and mental occurrences that enter into the human mind and brain: even though they may be unlimited, they can all still be retained there without that requiring any increase or decrease in the capacity and extent of the brain.

With regard to temporality, as well, a certain kind of extent of time takes place there that is unique for every particular individual being, varying according to their destiny and what they have come to deserve through their actions. Thus, according to the different individual cases, the period of one "year" in the intermediate world may not correspond at all to one year of solar time on the planet Earth, when you compare the two. For example, a full year of earthly time may be equivalent to as little as a second of time in the intermediate world.[14] And at the opposite extreme, a second of earthly time may correspond to as much as a year in the intermediate world.

Moreover, one should not suppose that the extent of periods of time in the intermediate world—for example, when it is mentioned that a single second there is equivalent to one year of solar time on earth, or the inverse—is the result of something illusory or unreal and imaginary. It is not at all like our imaginary seeing of things in a dream. For example, suppose that someone sees in a dream an enormous space filled with a vast multitude of people over an unimaginably immense period of time: yet when that person wakes up, nothing at all remains of the actual effects of those things. Whereas in that intermediate world, which is a world of (real) images or likenesses, the basis of space and time is solidly grounded in real spiritual sensations—not in the forms of size, number, and extension of this earthly, material world. Or to put it another way, *whatever appears to each person (in the intermediate world) through those spiritual sensations is actually real and absolutely true.*

Now the reason why the intermediate world has also been called a sort of "imaginal world" or "world of likenesses" is because after each being in this material, earthly world dies, it becomes manifest in the intermediate world in whatever shape and form and build it already had, with the same proportions and all its other qualities. Moreover, whatever milieu and surroundings it was lacking in this lower, material world for continuing its process of perfection, there will be prepared and projected for it in the intermediate world a real, particular milieu that is the exact likeness and image of the earthly milieu and surroundings that it needed, along with the period of time it needs. For example, if someone should die during childhood on earth, that person will experience the rest of their physical growth and development in the intermediate world. And the same sort of thing will appear for all other cases.

One final point that must also be considered attentively is that the difference between this lower, material world in relation to the higher realm of the intermediate world is exactly like the relation between (the state of) the fetus in its mother's womb and that of the newborn infant in its open, free environment, or like the difference that separates shadows from the light.

Of course this topic of the intermediate world (*barzakh*) has been sufficiently set forth in the Qur'an, the hadith (of the Prophet), the transmitted sayings (of the Imams) and in other religious books. For example,

1. In the Qur'an it is said (23:100): . . . *and behind them is a barzakh* (a distance and obstacle)[15] *until the Day they will be raised up.*

2. In the Qur'an commentary *al-Ṣāfī*,[16] it is reported that (the Imam) Ja'far al-Ṣādiq said: "The *barzakh* is something between

two other things, and it (refers to) the place of rewards and punishments between this world and the ultimate abode."[17]

3. In the "Fundamental Principles" section of the *Kāfī*,[18] it is reported from Imam Ja'far al-Sādiq that (he said): "All of you (my companions) are (destined for) the Garden and yet, by God, I fear for you in the *barzakh*!" Someone asked: "What is this *barzakh*?" He replied: "It is that abode which stretches from the moment of death until the Day of the Gathering."

In the *Majma' al-Bahrayn* it is also reported that Ja'far al-Sādiq said: "I fear for you because of the horrors of the *barzakh*. It lies between this lower world and the ultimate abode, from the moment of death until the Day of the Rising, so surely whoever dies enters the *barzakh*."

4. In the Arabic dictionary and in the *Majma' al-Bahrayn*, it is said that "a *barzakh* is a divider and boundary between two things. Between the time of death and the Rising, whoever dies enters it."[19]

Second Modality—the Process of Perfection through "Connection"
Between the Intermediate World and the Material World

The subjects included in this second modality, both the general principles and their particular applications, are exactly like those just mentioned in the preceding modality, with this one basic difference. (The proponents of this particular conception) say that the place where the necessary means will be prepared for those who have been kept from completing their process of perfection, so that they can make up for their imperfections, is right here in this lower, material world—the same place as their previous actions—instead of in the intermediate, imaginal world. This is because the place for harvesting whatever one has sown will be the same field where one did the sowing, in the following manner:

1. A direct spiritual connection is established for a specific period of time between the spirit that has stopped (in the course of its process of perfection) and is located in the intermediate world, and the spirit of another being here in this lower, material world; that period may be as long as the lifetime of the material body, or a shorter or longer period. This takes place by means of a spiritual connecting thread—comparable to the connection of an electrical circuit or the like— so that through it all of the pleasures and pains and educational experiences leading to spiritual perfection that occur to that bodily being (on

Earth) also have their direct effect on the other spirit in the intermediate world. This happens without the embodied spirit existing (on Earth) being aware of that connection or having any sensation of duality, since all the pleasures and pains and other experiences of that (earthly) bodily being are based on the determining factors of its own destiny.

In other words, the spirit in the intermediate world is able to make use of the sensations drawn from its ongoing connection with the spirit existing on Earth for its own process of perfection, according to the appropriate balance of factors relating to the process of perfection that are determined by God's Wisdom and determining Order, and in keeping with the essential spiritual potentiality of both the spirits involved. This is not the same as having two spirits in a single body, which is an impossibility. Such a direct spiritual connection is arranged so that the spirit in the intermediate world may be helped to attain and complete its own perfection. In any event, once the prescribed period of connection has run out, that spirit will be subject to the settling of its spiritual account in view of its eternal reward and recompense.

2. In establishing this connection between the spirit in the intermediate world and a bodily spirit on Earth, the two sides do not have to be of the same earthly gender and species. Indeed it is possible, depending on just what that particular spirit in the intermediate world has come to deserve because of its past actions, that it may be connected with a spirit having a material body like its own, or higher or lower. For example, a human being may be paired with another human, or a human with an animal, an animal with a human, and so on.

Third Modality: The Process of Perfection through "Accumulation"
(Of Influences from the Mineral, Vegetal, and Animal Levels of Existence) by Means of the Arc of Ascent

The proponents of this view explain it as follows:

First of all, as has already been mentioned several times in this book, the essential substance of each of the beings in the material world on the planet Earth—once that being has come into existence through the process of causality, thereby completing the arc of its (existentiating) descent from the Supreme Source to its lowest point, which is its initial emergence as a creature—must begin its corresponding arc of ascent from that lowest point back to the highest. Beginning there, that essential substance of each being must pass through the ascending stages of existence—for example, from the

mineral to the vegetal, then the animal stage—by means of the continuous transubstantial motion[20] of this arc of ascent, through the accu-
mulative combination (of influences from each of those lower stages of
existence), until it reaches the stage of the human-animal (*bashar*). (All
this takes place) in accordance with the particular demands of the (divine) Wisdom and the specific requirements of (each being's) nature,
which have been established in its created disposition by the Creator of
all creatures, through His inalterable particular determination.

Next, at the human-animal stage, once that being has become
adult, responsible, mature, and discerning (of good and evil), it must
pass through a thousand different spiritual stages until it arrives at—
or even merges with—the thousand-and-first stage,[21] which is the world
of Perfection and of reunion with the True One, the Reality of that
Point of (divine) Unicity and Singularity. But whenever that being
does not completely succeed in reaching those thousand specified stages
while still in its initial human form, then once it is transported to the
intermediate world, (it continues to learn) in those same ways that
were mentioned in *both* of the preceding sections in this chapter: either
by means of transposition from the material world into the intermediate world, or through the establishment of a spiritual connection
between (that being in) the intermediate world and (another creature)
in the material world. At that point, within the particular period allotted, it must completely fulfill its process of perfection—or otherwise
it will be subject to the settlement of its spiritual account and will
receive its eternal reward and recompense. We have alluded to the
views outlined in both the first and the second Modalities above because some people believe that the unfolding of the process of perfection takes place in the way described in the first Modality, while others
hold that the way described in the second Modality is correct. And *the
(true) Knowledge is with God!* (67:26).

Second, the arc of ascending movement of the beings from their
lowest stage, which the scholars in this field call the "mineral" stage—
for even if there are certain existent things lower than minerals, they
can be included under the "mineral" rubric—to the stage of plants
and then of animals does not take place in an individual manner. That
is, one shouldn't imagine that a particular individual from one of
those (lower) stages becomes transformed into another individual at a
level higher than itself; for example, a particular piece of rock will not
be transformed into the leaf of a plant, nor a leaf into an animal, nor
a single animal into an individual human being. That is because none
of those stages are equivalent to each other with regard to the relative
number of individuals or the extent of their lifetimes. It is inconceiv-

able that the many individual stones in the desert, each of which may last for many years in that same state, should be transformed into corresponding individual desert grasses that appear one spring and dry up and die that same autumn; or that each individual grass plant should become an individual animal, given the enormous differences between them in regard to both numbers and relative lifespans. Nor does it make any sense that individual animals—whether insects or others—should each be transformed into individual human beings, given that the numbers of the human species are so much fewer than the totality of all the other animals, while the human lifespan is greater than most of theirs. Indeed it could be said that, for example, the total number of human beings taken all together, from the first to the last, would not be equal to the numbers of even a single kind of insect, not to mention all the other animals. The same reasoning applies equally to the other levels of beings.

In consequence, the movements of the arc of ascent of the above-mentioned material things (i.e., minerals, animals, and plants) take place by means of changes that are gradual and continuous—like the movement of (a being) from its initial emergence until it reaches the completion of its bodily growth—and not by means of discontinuous changes involving transfer (from one individual to another). So one shouldn't imagine that the material constituents of the initial being are actually transferred into the matter of the next (higher being). Instead, it must be understood that the substantial life-source of mineral matter begins by undergoing the regular natural influences and the transformations resulting from this gradual, continuous process of change, passing through the various stages of its perfection, until it eventually reaches the final stage of potential for generating the material substrate of a plant. Then at that point, through the influence of the effusion of that generative life-source within it, a plant is generated and comes into existence. Likewise, it is through the successive gradual, natural transformations of the different individual minerals that soil comes into existence, and from that soil plants begin to grow. Then those plants, like the minerals, are transformed by their gradual, continuous process of change (in their substance) and pass through various stages until they reach the stage where the potential for generating an animal appears. Finally, the gradual, continuous process of transformation of the animal takes place in the same way until it reaches the stage of the human-animal (bashar).

To take a clearer image, the vital material influence of each of the above-mentioned material substances—whether mineral, vegetal, or animal—in bringing into existence the next higher substance is like the continual flow of water pouring out of a spring. In other words, as long as that water continues to flow ceaselessly from that source, then that continuously flowing stream, taken as a whole, could be considered to be one single thing: that is, the totality of all the particles of water from the source itself down to the end of that stream. Yet at the same time, considering the divisibility of that stream, each drop of it could also be considered a separate, individual thing. Thus it can be concluded that each one of the minerals and plants and animals, as long as they are alive, continuously and successively form a generative source for the material substance (of those higher beings) that come after them—just like the source of a continuously flowing stream—without a single material particle of their own being ever dissolving into the matter of the next one. As a result, the vital *influence* that passes from the initial material substance (of the first being) into the second one makes the second matter more perfect, because that second being then accumulates the influence from the first material substance together with the influences resulting from the natural conditions of its own material nature.

Thus in minerals it is only the influences of mineral (existences) that are accumulated, while plants contain the material influences of both minerals and plants, and animals contain the (accumulated material) influences of minerals, plants, and animals. As for human-animals (*bashar*), they contain the accumulated influences of those three material orders, as well as the influences of their own specifically human matter. The combined influences and material effects of that accumulated composite of constituent influences are indissoluble. It is somewhat like dissolving sugar in water, or similar phenomena—but with this basic difference that the sugar-water mixture can be separated by chemical means, whereas the accumulated composite of these vital life forces (in a given human being) cannot be separated.

In support of this view is the following statement reported by Kumayl[22] from Imam Ali. Kumayl said:

> I asked my master Ali: "Is there only one soul?" He replied:
> "O Kumayl, there are four souls: the vegetal, nutritive soul;
> the sensitive, animal soul; the rational, holy soul; and the
> universal, divine soul."

In another tradition (from Ali) it is reported:

> One of the desert Arabs asked about the soul, and Ali re-
> plied: "Which soul do you mean?" He responded: "O my
> master, is there more than one soul?" Then Ali answered:

"Yes indeed!" and he went on to enumerate the same four souls just mentioned.[23]

Third, when the appointed time is reached for the dissolution of the vital forces and the material elements of each individual being connected with these three realms of mineral, vegetal, and animal existence, they are returned to that primordial mineral matter of the planet Earth. It is self-evident that the planet Earth, since it is one of the heavenly bodies, has the same fate as the rest of the heavenly planetary bodies.

Fourth Modality—the "Unitive" Process of Perfection
By Means of the Two Arcs of Ascent and Descent

The point of view outlined in this modality, its proponents would say, is exactly the same as with those subjects that have just been mentioned in the preceding modality, with regard to the changes and transformations involved in the process of perfection through the mineral, vegetal, and animal realms of generation until reaching the stage of the human-animal (*bashar*). But from that point on, this is what they say: the human-animal is a composite of mineral, plant, animal, and human-animal material elements—but with the addition of an angelic, subtle, fully human (*insānī*) spirit that, according to the saying of Imam Ali,[24] is "the angelic, divine soul." [25]

Now we do not need to repeat here what was already said in chapter 2 by way of defining what the spirit is and just how it is created. Here the essential point to keep in mind is that since the spirit is something immaterial and devoid of matter, the bringing into existence of the spirit (by God) has no connection of any sort with the various kinds of matter involved in the generation of the body and (its organic) life, nor with the mixture of natural influences coming from minerals, plants, animals, and the human-animal (*bashar*). For the spirit is an exhalation of the Creator's Breath, as it says in the Qur'an: *I am indeed creating a human-animal (bashar) from clay. Then I rightly shaped him and I breathed into him from My own Spirit* . . . (15:28–29; 38:71–72). This is why the spirit has been compared to a sort of "subtle vapor," since it is neither visible nor tangible. Moreover, Ja'far al-Sādiq said: "The spirit is like a moving wind or breeze, and that is why it is called 'spirit' (*rūh*), because its name comes from the same root as 'wind' (*rīh*)."[26]

Thus the spirit is breathed into the human-animal (*bashar*) and becomes united with it at the time when the sixfold embryonic stages— of *extract* (of Clay), *droplet, clot, lump, bones,* and *flesh*—are completed, and it has become a full-fledged fetus.[27] This is supported by these words in the Qur'an: *Verily We have created the human being from an extract of Clay. Next We made him into a droplet in a secure resting place. Next We created from the droplet a clot of blood, then We created from the clot a lump of flesh, then We created bones from the lump of flesh, then We clothed the bones with flesh. After that We brought him into being in another creation.*[28] *So blessed be God, the Best of Creators!* (23:12–14).[29]

Besides, God's bringing the spirit into existence is not (necessarily) simultaneous with (the existence of) a body. Indeed, just as the spirit continues to exist after the disappearance of the body, likewise the spirit can also exist *before* the body[30]—or the two can come into existence simultaneously.

In any case, as was already mentioned in the third Modality (of the process of perfection) above, in order for the spirit to attain its perfection, one-thousand-and-one stages have been established. It must pass through one thousand of those stages in a human form, whether in its initial form or in subsequent successive forms, through what is called "the process of perfection," until it reaches its reunion with God, the Truly Real, in the thousand-and-first stage, and becomes eternally blessed in the abode of the hereafter.

Since this is the case, if a spirit is able to attain its perfection in its first human form, by dint of its own effort and striving and exertion—or through special divine assistance—then it has reached its desired goal. But if it is not able to complete its process of perfection and pass through its thousand spiritual stages in that first human form—whether that be because of carelessness, laziness, going astray, or any other obstacles—and must therefore come back again in subsequent, successive human forms, that should not be interpreted as implying transmigration.[31] Absolutely none of the arguments that the philosophers, sages, and learned scholars have advanced to show the falsity of that theory (of transmigration) apply to the process of spiritual perfection in the sense that has just been mentioned and that is further explained below. For there is a total opposition between the proponents of this form of the process of perfection and those who argue for transmigration.[32] Therefore in order to clarify the matter for those seeking (the truth about this matter), the arguments for the falsity of the belief in transmigration will be explained, God willing, in their appropriate place (in chapter 8).

At this point, however, in order not to interrupt the discussion of this subject, we will set forth the following remaining topics connected with this "unitive" form of the process of perfection:

1. The maximum period allotted for passing through the different stages of spiritual perfection is *fifty thousand years* (70:4), calculated according to the years of the planet Earth's orbit in the solar system.

The minimum period (for completing that spiritual process) is the lifespan of the initial human form.

2. Within that fifty thousand years, the average lifespan in each human form is approximately fifty years.

3. If, for example, (a spirit's) lifespan is a hundred years or more in one human form, then in subsequent lives it will have a shorter lifetime so that the average lifespan will remain fifty years per lifetime.

4. From the maximum period of fifty thousand years allotted for passing through the stages (of the process of spiritual perfection) in different human bodies, we may conclude that at least a thousand human forms are allotted (for each spirit to reach its perfection).

5. Once (a spirit has been born) in a human body, it must live, at the very least, for a period of forty full days after leaving the mother's womb. Otherwise, even if it lives for just a second less than forty days, that lifetime is not counted in the succession of the thousand spiritual stages and the thousand human forms allotted for its process of perfection. In fact, that will be considered as a kind of penalty.

6. If (a spirit), as a result of a degradation in its spiritual rank, must be connected with bodies lower than human bodies, then that period is not included in its accounting (of the allotted period) for the process of perfection, no matter how numerous those bodies may be or how long it may spend (in that lower condition).

7. Whenever a spirit does not succeed in completing the thousand spiritual stages of the process of perfection within its allotted period of fifty thousand years and through its thousand human forms, then it will remain forever deprived of the grace of the spiritual rank of Perfection—that is, of its reunion with God, the Truly Real. However, it will be given a reward for its good deeds, in accordance with what it has come to deserve, in one of the (spiritual) levels below the station of Perfection. Or it will receive the appropriate retribution for its evil deeds—which is a particular form of shame and suffering, either temporary or permanent—in one of the lower spiritual levels or even the *"lowest of the low,"* as it is mentioned in the Qur'an:

> *Certainly We created the human being in the best of forms. Then We returned him to the lowest of the low, except for those who have faith and do what is right: for theirs is a reward without restriction. So after that what would cause you to deny (God's) Religion/Judgment? Is God not the Wisest of those who judge?!* (95:4–8)

In other words—apart from the (highest) station of Perfection, which is (the spirit's) conjoining with the point of Unicity of the True

Reality—all the other spiritual stations and rewards and punishments for the good and bad deeds of each person, which are in accordance with what each one deserves, descend from the station of the loftiest of *"Heights"* to the *"lowest of the low."* This is likewise as it is stated in the Qur'an: *Most certainly, the Book* (of actions) *of the wicked is in the frightful Prison!* And: *Most certainly, the Book* (of deeds) *of the upright is in the blessed Heights!* (23:7, 18).[33]

8. As for the spirit that has not yet reached the stage of spiritual Perfection, after each of its lifetimes it exchanges its bodily form, dying and then coming back to life. However each time it dies, once that spirit separates from its physical body, the body disintegrates, while that spirit survives and is transported to the intermediate world for a certain time.

9. The period the spirit remains in the intermediate world is not determined in advance, and is not the same for everyone. Thus some spirits are returned to another material, earthly form almost immediately, while others remain there (in the intermediate, spiritual world) for a certain period. This is because the greater or lesser length of each spirit's stay in the intermediate world is based on a specific *Reckoning* that is determined by the true Keeper of accounts in that world.

10. The process of the spirit's leaving its initial human form and subsequently entering into other successive human forms has been called, in the technical language of this group, the movement from "garment to garment" or "turn to turn" or "manifestation to manifestation."[34] According to their opinion, this process is alluded to in the following verse from the Qur'an: . . . *Whenever their skins are cooked* [or *"completed"*], *We exchange them for those people with other skins . . .* (4:56).

11. All of the creatures endowed with a spirit on the planet Earth, in accordance with the Wisdom of nature and with their essential created disposition, fall into three groups: the first and second groups are those who are truly (entirely) either male or female,[35] who remain as they are in every bodily form and matter. The third group is the androgynous category, who by their original essential nature possess the aptitude and potentiality that fall between the other two groups. That is, they can become truly male or female, either in this bodily form or in other later forms, as a result of particular changes or accidental causes; or they may remain indefinitely in this androgynous condition. As can be seen in some cases, the sexual identities of some people do change after a certain period.

12. If a human spirit should descend to being (connected with) an animal,[36] it will appear in those higher animals that possess a certain power of reflection, not just any animal.

13. Given that the human, angelic spirit (*rūh-i malakūtī-yi insānī*) does not depend upon the contingent, human-animal (*bashar*) soul of the naturally composite body, it is possible that the spirit of one individual may be exchanged for another spirit during his lifetime, without that person even being aware of that exchange; this can happen by God's command, due to some particular wisdom or benefit, or as the result of certain deeds. Some of the mystical thinkers, such as Shaykh Nasafī and others,[37] called that (new spirit) a "suddenly appearing" spirit, because it suddenly appears in an already living body. Still others call such a spirit an "imaginal" spirit, because they say it is like the imaginal apparition of the Holy Spirit to the Prophet in the form of Dahyā al-Kalbī, or the way the angelic spirit (of Gabriel) took on the imaginal appearance of a mortal human form for the Virgin Mary, as indicated in the Qur'an: *So she chose seclusion far from them. Then We sent to her Our Spirit, and he took the appearance for her of a well-formed man* (19:18).

14. The inequalities between people[38] that each creature encounters in the course of life, in every respect and in every sense, whatever their name or description, are always based upon a detailed and precise accounting of the consequences of each creature's previous and current and future actions, or on (the particular conditions of) that being's own process of perfection. For God is Just and His overflowing Grace is universal.

15. It has already been mentioned that the spirit of every human being who has not, in their initial human bodily form, passed through the thousand spiritual stages of the process of perfection in order to reach the stage of Perfection, of the Truly Real, must be brought back again and again in other human bodily forms until they complete their allotted period (for this process of spiritual perfection). Now a necessary consequence of this process would be that the person should not forget in each new bodily form those thoughts and earlier events that have had an effect upon their spirit in their preceding bodily forms. Yet in fact, apart from three exceptional instances that will soon be discussed, no one is ordinarily aware of the events and happenings of their own past bodily forms. That is why the experts in this matter have mentioned by way of explanation the following three points:

First Point: The spirit itself is incorporeal, unbounded by material limits. So whenever it is dwelling in the other world, without the body and bodily life of a human-animal form, none of the events and happenings from its earlier successive bodily lifetimes are hidden from it. Indeed certain of the predestined conditions of its future are also not concealed from it.

However, whenever the spirit is located in a human form, in accordance with the demands of nature, it is obscured by a veil of forgetfulness between the present and its past, due to its being overcome by the body's materiality and the passions of the domineering self (*nafs*). In addition, since the body and bodily life and perceptions of each individual in each particular bodily form are different from those of all its other previous bodily forms, it is evident that whatever had been registered by the faculty of memory in each of its preceding bodily forms disappears, like all of the other bodily faculties, along with each of those bodily forms. However, those things *are* recorded by the spirit in the other world, as was indicated above.

Second Point: If the veil of forgetfulness between present occurrences and earlier events were not established at the beginning of each new bodily form, it is obvious that memories present, past, and yet to come would all be joined together as a single memory. But in that case the matter of the thousand spiritual stages to be passed through in the process of perfection would disappear, and the necessary opportunities for passing through the ups and downs of the different stages of the process of perfection would no longer exist.

Third Point: If a consciousness of earlier experiences (in other lives) did remain (in this life), then it might happen that the old relationships between persons who had had either good or bad relations in their earlier human forms would again be restored. That could lead to a breakdown of the social order, or to such disturbing and upsetting relations between the different parties that their own process of perfection would be interrupted.

However that may be, it should be noted that in general each of the above-mentioned points may be taken to be either entirely or partially valid in itself, and that other relevant considerations could also be envisaged. Or else this might be considered one of those "secrets hidden" (with God), because there truly are so many secrets in the world of the Unseen that far surpass the capacity of understanding of human beings and all the other creatures—which indeed can only be grasped within God's Knowledge. With that in mind, only this much is certain: that the ultimate cause for people's ignorance of their own earlier experiences, whatever that might be, is based on God's providential arranging of all things for the best. For it is quite clear that the Creator's Will and providential arrangement of things is never without its underlying Wisdom and purpose.

As for the three exceptions (to this general forgetfulness of one's previous lives) already alluded to above, first of all it must be understood *that it is not the material body in itself that causes the veil of*

forgetfulness keeping us from an awareness of our earlier experiences.
Rather, it is the passions of the domineering self that bring that veil
of obscurity into existence. Thus, to the extent that the spirit is able to
free itself from the bonds of illusions created by the passions, the
thickness of its veil of unconsciousness will be reduced to that same
degree. That is why certain individuals are able to perceive a true
vision of things from the past or the future at the time when the bodily
powers are asleep and the spirit is set free. This is the basic principle
by which we should understand the following exceptional cases, as
they are explained by the leaders of this group (i.e., the proponents of
the gradual perfection of the spirit) regarding this matter:

First Exception: Every human being remembers certain memories from his or her past, either completely or partially, from the point
of birth onward for a certain specific period. That period extends for
at least forty days, but its maximum extent differs according to each
individual's spiritual potential, and is therefore indeterminate. This is
how thoughtful people have understood this exception:

(a) Every newborn infant of the human species, after it has been
born from the mother's womb and the spirit has been breathed into it,
will recall memories of its past for a certain period, as long as that
infant has not completed the natural development of its power of
thought and its voluntary motions, such as gesturing, making signs,
speaking, and so on. This is because at that age it cannot yet distinguish between the self associated with its new bodily form and the
self of its former bodily form. As a result of that, it is still living in the
dreamlike state of its past, like the dream of someone who is sleeping.
Then those earlier experiences are gradually erased from its memory,
as its bodily and mental powers develop. Of course the period during
which it remembers that preceding existence is very short: it may not
exceed a few months at most.

(b) Among these newborn infants, there are some rare individuals
who do not forget some of the memories of their preceding bodily form
at any age, due to a power of memory that is located beyond the brain;
this is because of certain contributing factors of their constitution.

Second Exception: In connection with the above-mentioned points
6 and 12 regarding the process of spiritual perfection, every human
being that is connected to an animal form as a result of its state being
lowered (as a special punishment) is reminded—as long as it remains
connected to that animal form—of certain exceptional memories (of
misdeeds) from its last human form that deserve condemnation or
reproof, by way of punishment and awakening its awareness. Its "being reminded" refers to the fact that since the animal level is lower

than the human level, those causes that bring about the veiling (of memories of the preceding lifetime) in human beings are weaker in the animal, due to its more limited power of thinking and perception. This means that such a person is reminded of whatever has to do with their punishment and their being brought to awareness (of their wrong-doing), not of all their preceding experiences.

Third Exception: This happens for every human being who has accumulated exceptional (good deeds) in their preceding bodily forms and has devoted all of this life to good thoughts, good words, and good actions, seeking God's Satisfaction throughout all the stages of their life in this current bodily form—especially if they have become liberated from all the attachments of this world, so that even memories of the pleasures and pains of their previous bodily forms no longer have any power over them. Such individuals, due to their spirit's control over their (domineering, human-animal) soul and to the completely polished state of the mirror of their being, are able to recall their experiences in past lives, to the extent of their own individual capacity.

Now we have sufficiently completed the discussion of the four dimensions of the process of spiritual perfection.

A (Final) Illuminating Remark

Of course what is involved in the rewarding and punishing of each human being's good and bad actions on the Day of Gathering has not been left unmentioned in the course of all the preceding discussions. In addition, the essentials of that subject have been clearly explained and set forth in detail and made accessible to everyone, for those who are seeking (the truly divine) Religion, by means of the religious scriptures revealed through the prophets sent on behalf of the *Lord of the worlds* (1:2). However, it may still be useful to mention in this book the following illuminating remark by way of helping people to understand this question.

First, *there are two kinds of reward and punishment for every person's good and bad actions: one of them is the consequences of that action here in this world, and the other is the reward or punishment of that action in the other (spiritual) world.* For example, if someone performs a useful service or an act of selfless love, or helps other individuals or society without any recompense, then the consequence of their action is that they will earn the respect, esteem, love, and good opinion of others. And they will also have their (spiritual) reward in the realm of the Return. But if someone commits a bad deed, its consequence is precisely the humiliation, opprobrium, disgust, scorn, and other misfortunes they encounter in the realm of this world; that person will also experience the corresponding punishment on the Day of Judgment.

In other words, *every action will have an immediate (this-worldly) effect and an ultimate (spiritual) result.*

Second, with regard to each of the above-mentioned (good or bad) actions committed by every individual, a specific, impartial reward or punishment is known and carried out, which is determined in accordance with the scales and balances of the calculations of divine Justice. This is subject to the condition that *God Almighty, in keeping with the gracious Bounty and Goodness of His Caring for His servants, will reward (each good action) ten times over; while in accordance with the Justice of His judgment, (each bad action) will receive a single punishment.* As it says in the Qur'an: *Whoever performs a good deed will receive ten times its like; and whoever does an evil deed will only receive the recompense of its like. For no injustice will be done to them!* (6:160).

Third, the quantities and the distinctive qualities of the actual pleasures and the pains of the eternal realm of the Return are inconceivable. For each of the levels of the blessings of paradise and the sufferings of hell, of their respective "gardens" and "fires," are always described through likenesses and symbols designed to be understandable to human beings, to help them understand and become aware in general terms of the reality of the existence of the rewards and punishments that exist in that realm. Otherwise, the degree of intensity of the effect of each of those blessings and punishments in that realm are such that they could not even be compared with what can be imagined here. To put it simply, until you've actually tasted them, you just can't know! We can only recognize the specific flavor of each food by actually tasting it, not by putting together a verbal description of it. For example, the word "sweet" covers all sorts of sweet things, such as sugar, honey, dates, raisins, and so on, yet the ability to recognize the distinctive quality of sweetness of each of them comes through actual tasting, not by talking about them.

Fourth, the "eternal" punishments that persons may receive in the afterlife are at the time after each person's allotted period of "Proof"[39] in this world has been completed. This refers to that period that the Creator has actually allowed for completing the Proof (of each spirit's process of perfection), not to whatever a creature might consider that period to be. Thus in the case of someone who fails to complete their Proof in their initial human body, their allotted period is not yet completed at that point. Since God is both *the Most Merciful of the merciful ones* (12:64) and truly Just, He will allow this Proof to be

fully accomplished for that person through the appropriate means of
the intermediate world or through the larger process of perfection.
Only then will that person receive the set punishments.

Chapter Eight

The Belief of the Proponents of Transmigration

The belief of the proponents of transmigration concerning the spirit[1]—
which they also call "the soul"[2]—is as follows:

First, at the moment of death and the decay and disappearance
of the body, the spirit of every being that exists in each body in this
material world must be transferred to another elemental body, different and separate from that first body, in the same material dimension
of this world.

Second, the transfer of that initial spirit to another material body
must take place without any delay or interruption.

Third, it is necessary that the connection be instantaneous, without any pause or interval of delay or advance, between the time of
death of the body of the first being and the time of establishing the
existence of the second being with whose body that initial spirit will
then become connected.

Fourth, the proponents of this belief maintain that there is absolutely no beginning or end to these movements of the spirit, no starting point or limit, no origin and no goal, no purpose or aim. They say
that every being must continue throughout eternity in this state of
constant transferal from one body to another.

Fifth, in the opinion of this group, there is no sense in talking
about a Return or any rewards and punishments at a (Day of) Rising.

They believe that any justice and equity and balancing out of the consequences of actions will take place *only in this world*, by means of those ongoing transfers (from one body to another). In other words, if a spirit commits a good or bad action in one body, then it will reap the fruits of that action in one or more subsequent bodies.

Sixth, the proponents of transmigration are divided into several schools, including the following groups:

(a) The school of "replacement": this group maintains that the transferal of a human spirit after the death and decay of the body is (only) to another *human* body. They call this the process of "replacement" (*naskh*).[3]

(b) The school of "metamorphosis" (into animals): this group claims that the transferal of the human spirit after death is to the bodies of various animals—including higher animals, insects, and others—in accordance with the moral qualities of the good and bad actions of each spirit when it was in a human body. Thus, for example, (the spirits of) greedy individuals may be trans- ferred into ants or pigs, or those of thieves may become mice, crows, and the like. They call this the process of "metamorpho- sis" or "zöomorphosis" (*maskh*).

(c) The school of "dissolution": they are like the preceding group, except that they extend the process of transferal (of human spir- its) to the realm of plants, including trees, herbs, and others. This they call the process of "dissolution" (*faskh*).

(d) The school of "implantation:" this sect shares the opinions of the two preceding groups, with the exception that they extend the transferal of human spirits after death to include as well the whole mineral realm, including rocks, soil, and so on. This is what they call the process of "solidification" (*raskh*).

The late Hajj Mulla Hādī Sabzavārī, in his book the *Manzūmah*,[4] says (by way of summarizing these four groups af- firming *tanāsukh*): "Replacement, metamorphosis, dissolution, so- lidification: they are divided according to (transferal into) humans, animals, minerals, and plants."

(e) Still another group are called the "proponents of ascension": some people consider them a fifth sect among the transmigrationists, while others would include them among those who argue for the process of spiritual perfection. In any case, this group, unlike the preceding four groups, maintain that the soul's transferal—or the process of the spirit's perfection—takes place in an *ascending* direction, not through any descent (into lower realms of existence). Thus they say: "The vegetal soul is gradually transferred from lower to higher levels of existence until it reaches a body among the lowest animal levels. Then it is gradually transferred in the same way from the lower to the nobler levels of animals until it enters the body of a human being. Likewise the human spirit is transferred after death into heavenly bodies."

Next, keeping in mind the above-mentioned different groups of those who believe in transmigration, we will give here a summary of the arguments that the learned experts in this domain have established in order to demonstrate the *falsity* of these schools, so that those desiring to verify this can judge for themselves.

1. The consensus of the people of the different religious communities has upheld the falsity of this opinion, especially since an essential principle in the religion of Islam and the other religions is the belief in the (spirit's) Return (to its divine Source)—whether that Return be conceived as physical, spiritual, or other.

2. It is not correct that the soul, when it gives up the governance of a particular body because of the corruption of that bodily constitution and that body's inability to receive its control, is (automatically) transferred to another natural body in this same this-worldly dimension, because that would entail a false consequence. That is because every body, at the beginning of its establishment, must have a certain preparedness or potential. Only after that (bodily) preparedness is completed and it has attained the constituents of its specific bodily constitution through the completion of the causality (exercised by) the Primordial Ultimate Cause, is a connection established between that body and a *new* soul coming from the Necessary Being, Who is the Bestower of the governing souls, without any delay or interruption. In other words, every body whose preparedness and receptivity (for having a soul) becomes complete—through the whole process of causes and effects originating with the original Ultimate Cause, which is the Essence of the Necessary Being—is then immediately connected with a new governing soul, without any waiting or interruption.

Now in this case, if a sort of collision were to ensue between the "transferred" soul (as claimed by the transmigrationists) and the newly arriving (created) soul just mentioned, then in that case there would necessarily have to be a conjunction of two different souls in a single body. But (the impossibility of this happening clearly illustrates the logical rule that) "when the necessitating principle is false, then its consequence is also false." For it is one of the laws of nature that each body has *only one* new soul. Indeed it is also logically impossible for two essentially independent souls, one of them new and the other transferred, to be received and conjoined in a single body. (In such a case) we must suppose that the transferred, transmigrating soul would prevent the arrival of that newly (created) soul in the body to which it is transferred, or else that the new soul would somehow be dissolved or absorbed in that transmigrating soul. But that would be illogical and without any rational basis, since neither of those two souls would have the sort of priority or preference (entitling it) to prevent or absorb the other one. Thus, as has already been stated, the conjunction of two souls in a single body must be judged to be false.

3. The connection between a (particular) soul and body is an *essential* connection: there is always a unitary, natural, constitutive combination between the two that continually operates throughout their various states and all their transformations in (the categories of) quantity and quality. In other words, this soul is already something (that exists) *potentially* even at the beginning of the origin and development of a particular being, just as that body already has a potential connection with that (particular) soul. Thus both the body and soul (of a given particular being) are always joined together, by means of the gradual, essential motions and changes of that (single) substance, as they pass through the stages of the ascending and descending movements of those bodily and spiritual powers. For example, they support and sustain each other through all the states (of that particular being), both spiritual and bodily, from the stage of the embryo and fetus until the completion of that being's arc of growth and ascent in adolescence, and subsequently throughout the course of the descending arc until old age and the moment of that body's death and decay and dissolution. Through all of those states, that being develops both spiritually and bodily together. Thus, through the strengthening and constitutive interaction of their respective powers, they (body and spirit together) bring into actual existence what was only potential within them.

So it is only after death that the body will pass away and the spirit will survive independently and eternally. Therefore (if one were to grant the transmigrationists' theory), there is an obvious conflict and inherent contradiction between the "transferred" soul that has already moved from a potential to an actualized state, and the newly originated soul, which has not yet moved from its potential to full actualization. Hence from this perspective as well, the combination and cooperation of those two souls (in a single body) is both really and logically impossible.

4. As has already been mentioned, the proponents of transmigration maintain that it is impossible for there to be any lapse of time or period of interruption during the transferal of the original spirit (from one body) into a second body. Yet the fact is that there must necessarily be some moment of time, however short, between the time the soul separates from its first body and the time it is transferred into its new body. This also points to the falseness of their view.

5. According to the school of transmigration propounded by the ancient sages of Babylonia, Iran, and the Buddha,[5] the connection between the time of the death of the first (bodily) being and the time of the actualization of the second being (in which the soul comes to exist) takes place as follows:

The first point of descent (of the human soul) is a "ruling light of the human castle."[133] In other words, the first stage of the coming down of the immaterial substance of the soul is in this *human* body, with its complete range of faculties. Thus they consider the human body to be the original source and gateway for the (subsequent) lives of all of the elemental bodies of the animals on earth, in the sense that human souls, after death and their separation from their earthly, material bodies, are divided into one of the following groups:[7]

- First, there are the blessed, perfected ones who are immediately transferred to the noetic World of Light and are eternally joined with the (angelic) *Loftiest Assembly* (38:69).

- Second, there are those blessed ones who have not attained perfection, who may be considered an intermediate, (spiritually) incomplete group. Thus, according to the corresponding merits of their (good or bad) actions and moral qualities, (their souls) may be transferred—according to their higher or lower rank—into the bodies of other human beings, or into the bodies of noble or relatively higher animals.

- Third, there is the group of *the wretched* (87:11), those who, in accordance with the relative degree of intensity or weakness of the punishment for their (evil) deeds, are transferred to the bodies of lower animals corresponding to their dominant moral traits while in their human bodies, such as predatory, vicious, or harmful creatures, or into the bodies of lowly, downward-gazing animals, such as pigs and the like.

Now the reasons for the falsity of these above-mentioned beliefs include the following:

To begin with, on the assumption that there is no connection (of the soul with a body) between the time of death of the first being's body and the time of readiness of (the body of) a second being, there will necessarily be a period of delay and interruption. But one of the basic premises (shared by all the philosophers) is that existence does not allow for such an interruption.

Second, the supposedly self-evident "necessity" requiring an immediate connection (of soul-transfer) between the time of death of the human body and the time of readiness of a second living being (to receive that soul) hasn't been proven or established at all! Indeed it would appear that it cannot be verified. So although it might be verifiable somewhere—for example, in the purely spiritual world—all we have here is an arbitrary supposition of such a necessary (immediate soul-transfer) connection, a mere assertion without any proof. So "it is up to the claimant to prove it."

The third reason is that even if we suppose that there is a necessary connection between the time of death of a (particular) human body and the time of readiness of the other beings (to receive that human soul), then that would still imply that the number of (newly ready) animal bodies on the earth must be equal to the actual number of deaths of human bodies. That is because (given that supposition, one of the following cases must apply):

- If the number of dying human bodies is greater than the number of (newly) existing animal bodies, then that would require the combining of several (previously) human souls in a single animal body. Now the fallacious consequence of this would be that if there were nothing to prevent the combining of several souls in that single body, then that would bring about disorder in their governing of that body, which is contrary to the necessity for order and the proper natural functioning of organisms. For each individual body cannot have more than one soul governing it. But if the body does have an influence in preventing and stopping that combination (of several souls within it), then the combination of those souls, or at least of some of them, would become useless—and it is not possible for anything in existence to be useless, as has already been indicated. For all of the specialists in this field (of natural philosophy) are agreed that "there is nothing useless in existence."

- And if the number of animals (newly) existing is greater than the number of dying human bodies, then in that case whenever a single human soul became connected to the bodies of a number of animals, each of those animals in itself would also *be* other than itself (since that soul is what gives the bodies their identity). For example, that animal that ought to be connected with the soul of Zayd would also be connected (through that single soul) with a number of other animals—which goes counter to all reason and logic.

- But if that single (human-transferring) soul only became connected to a single (new animal) body, while all the other newly emerging animal bodies each took on a *newly originated* soul, then in any event there would be no deciding reason for that connection happening to one of those bodies rather than any of the others. While if, on the other hand, new souls did not become connected with those newly emerging animal bodies, then those bodies would remain soulless and uselessly inactive—which is also impossible.

Moreover, what we can witness directly and firsthand, with our own senses, is that undoubtedly most of the time there would be incomparably more newly developing kinds of (animal) beings—including all the mammals, reptiles, and insects on the earth—than dying members of the human species. For example, in a single day so many more ants or gnats or sea animals—especially in the genera of fish—come into being, by far, than the number of human beings who die over many years. So on the basis of this principle, the falsity of the belief of the proponents of transmigration becomes quite clear.

6. As for what the transmigrationists say by way of denying any beginning or end for the various transferals of the souls, that also has (self-evidently) false implications. That is because everything that exists—apart from God Almighty, Who has no beginning or end—must have a start and a finish, a source and a place of Return, a specific goal. Otherwise we are forced to refer to (all beings') "seeking what is absolutely unknowable"—and whether it be in spiritual matters or the things of this world, that sort of belief and approach is illogical and pointless.

7. As for what the transmigrationists say by way of denying any rewards and punishments and (moral) Reckoning and ultimate Justice in an eternal realm of Return, that also has a great many false implications, including the following points:

- First, all of the religions of the people of the (revealed) Scriptures believe in the Return (of the individual souls) and a final Reckoning (for their good and bad deeds).

- Secondly, it is a rational conclusion that if the eternal (realm of the) Return does not exist, then there is also no immortality of the (individual) spirit. And if there is no survival of the spirit, then they really agree with the words of the pure materialists,[8] that "what dies is completely gone." However, this will also result in undermining the foundational beliefs (maintaining) human society, since someone who doesn't believe in the (soul's) Return will not refrain from those (socially destructive) actions that are prohibited.

- In any case, (the transmigrationists' insistence on) all those movements of the spirit from one body to another body actually presuppose this (immortality of the spirit). For if that spirit does not survive, then the very subject of discussion disappears and becomes pointless.

There are many more arguments for the falsity of the belief of the proponents of transmigration, in addition to those mentioned here. However it would seem that these should be sufficient for people with intelligence and good judgment.[9] Of course it should be mentioned as well that the supporters of transmigration have also given their responses supporting their claims and refuting or raising doubts about the arguments of those maintaining the falsity of transmigration. Yet since all of those doubts and sophistical arguments have been repeatedly refuted and rejected by the learned specialists in this field, there should be no need to record them all here, especially since their detailed discussion would take us beyond the intended limits of this book, which is based on a summary approach.

Conclusion

This marks the conclusion of the book *Knowing the Spirit*. Because God Almighty has granted this poor servant, Nur Ali Elahi, the grace of successfully completing its composition, I thank and praise Him both in speech and with all my heart! In addition, I ask my esteemed readers to please forgive any mistakes, errors, oversights, or inaccuracies that they may discover in the writing of this work, since my stock of learning was only sufficient for this much.

Indeed it should be noted that whatever has been recalled in this book concerning the different aspects of the metaphysical world— including the realm of the (spirit's) Return, the process of spiritual perfection, and others—has been drawn from the transmitted words of the truly competent authorities, not from any personal belief. For just as we mentioned in the introduction to this book, no one but God knows the secrets of that realm. As it says in the Qur'an:

> *And the keys of the Unseen are with Him: no one knows them but Him!* (6:59)

Or as it also says:

> *Say: "No one who is in the heavens and the earth knows the Unseen but God"—nor do they know when they are being raised up.* (27:65)

So it should be obvious that any difficulties or objections that people of learning may encounter with regard to these subjects should not be held against the author.

> *And Peace be with whoever follows the right Guidance!* (20:47)

—Completed April 30, 1968, Nur Ali Elahi

115

Notes to the Translator's Introduction

1. Following Ostad Elahi's own explicit practice (and the scriptural sources and references shared by all the Abrahamic traditions), which intentionally highlights the universality, immortality, and divine origin of the life principle in question across all its outwardly different manifestations (see chapter 2 of *Knowing the Spirit*), I have consistently translated *rūh* as "spirit" throughout this work. The much more ambiguous term "soul" has been reserved to translate the Arabic term *nafs* ("self," as well as "soul"), which the author normally mentions here *only* when citing the language and arguments of various groups of Islamic philosophers who did not normally speak of the "spirit" (especially in chapters 2 and 8). Even in the restricted case of human beings, as specified in a key citation from Imam 'Ali in the third modality section of chapter 7, the term *nafs* can normally refer to four *different* dimensions of the human self—including the vegetal, animal, and "human-animal" (*bashar*) composite souls, in addition to that particular "divine, angelic" (*malakūtī*) element that is the immortal *spirit* and the primary subject of this book. See also Ostad Elahi's further development of this basic distinction, especially his unambiguously clear distinction of the angelic "truly human" (*insānī*) spirit from the lower "human-animal" (*bashar*) and other lower "souls" (*nafs*) in point 13 of the fourth modality section of chapter 7.

2. I should also note that the author's extremely detailed table of contents (given in full at the beginning of the translation of *Knowing the Spirit*) provides another useful means of following his overall argument and the place of particular discussions in relation to his guiding intentions.

3. In other words, *connaissance* not *savoir*: *ma'rifa* is the standard technical term used for realized spiritual awareness in all the later traditions of Islamic spirituality and mysticism. Paradoxically, most of this work is literally formulated in the complex abstract terminology of the traditional forms of philosophical and religious learning (*'ilm*, primarily in Arabic-language writings) familiar to Ostad Elahi's original scholarly audience, and it is the key

assumptions and procedures of those unfamiliar learned disciplines that are explained to modern readers in section 2 of the introduction.

4. Almost all writings and publications in recent decades now use the shorter honorific, Ostad Elahi. The most detailed biographical study to date, focusing primarily on Ostad Elahi's accomplishments as a musician, is certainly Jean During's recent *L'Âme des sons: L'art unique d'Ostad Elahi (1895–1974)* (Gordes: Editions le Relié, 2001). In addition, one of my PhD students is now preparing a biographical study focusing on Ostad Elahi's juridical career and related ethical and social teachings.

A great deal of additional biographical information, including a wealth of photographs from all periods of Ostad Elahi's life and accounts by people who had known him personally, was brought together in the volume entitled *Unicity* (Paris: Robert Laffont, 1995), prepared for the international UNESCO-sponsored commemoration of the centenary of his birth in 1995. Especially important, from a biographical perspective, was the extensive collection of materials relating to his life (including his library, musical instruments, CDs of his music, videos, etc.) assembled for the commemorative exposition held at the Sorbonne in that year. Much of that exposition material is still accessible at the bilingual website established on that occasion (www.ostadelahi.com).

Additional helpful biographical references—including ongoing lecture, concert, and seminar series on Ostad Elahi and his teachings—can be found on the following closely related websites (all with English-language versions): www.fondationostadelahi.org; www.nourfoundation.com; and www.saintjani.org. The latter site is devoted to his younger sister, Malek Jān (better known by her nickname "Jānī"), 1906–1993, who became an influential and highly revered spiritual figure in her own right.

5. Those sayings and spiritual teachings were recorded by his students and eventually published in the two massive volumes entitled *Athār al-Haqq* (*Traces of the Truth*), ed. Bahram Elahi, volume I (Tāhūrī, 1978) and volume II (Jayhūn, 1992). The sayings quoted later are all drawn from these two volumes; the quotations cited here are mainly from the autobiographical chapter 24 of volume I, identified by their number in that volume.

Two short collections of Ostad Elahi's translated sayings excerpted from *Athār al-Haqq* in highly abridged form were published, in both English and French, on the occasion of the 1995 centenary celebrations: *100 Maxims of Guidance*, by Ostad Elahi, and *Words of Faith: Prayers of Ostad Elahi* (both Paris: Robert Laffont, 1995).

6. Ostad Elahi's discussions of the extraordinary spiritual personality of his father are concentrated in chapter 23 of *Athār al-Haqq* (vol. 1), as well as in many of the stories recounted in chapter 24. Although his family grew up in a remote Kurdish area of western Iran, "Hajjī Ni'mat," as he was familiarly known, was one of the main spiritual teachers memorably described early in Gurdjieff's famous *Meetings with Remarkable Men*. (Another of my PhD students in Paris is now preparing a pioneering study of Hajjī Ni'mat, including an edition of part of his own autobiographical account of his remarkable, original spiritual illumination.)

7. *Shāhnāmeh-ye Haqīqat*, a Persian (and Kurdish) mystical epic poem of more than 15,000 lines, edited by H. Corbin, in the collection Bibliothèque Iranienne (Tehran and Paris: Institut Français, 1966), as well as in the subsequent corrected edition and commentary by Ostad Elahi (*Haqq al-Haqā'iq*) discussed at the end of this biographical section (see note 13).

8. *Athār al-Haqq*, vol. 1, saying no. 1873. Subsequent sayings quoted from that work are identified simply by their reference number (in parentheses after the saying).

9. For a detailed study of Ostad Elahi's remarkable music and its spiritual effects and significance, see the recent book by Jean During (*L'Âme des sons . . .*) in note 4. Professor During and Dr. Shahrokh Elahi (Ostad Elahi's youngest son, in whom he confided much of his musical knowledge) have cooperated in the recent preparation and publication of a series of widely accessible CD versions of recordings of Ostad Elahi's music made late in his life.

10. *Burhān al-Haqq* (*Demonstration of the Truth*) (1st edition, Tehran: 1963; 7th edition, 1985); *Ma'rifat ar-Rūh* (*Knowing the Spirit*) (1st edition, Tehran: 1969; 4th edition, 1992); and *Haqq al-Haqā'iq*, his commentary and corrected edition of his father's long poem, *Shāhnāmeh-ye Haqīqat* (Tehran: 1969).

11. See the full references to *Athār al-Haqq* at note 5; the 1,200 pages of these two volumes alone would correspond to at least ten volumes in an adequately annotated, complete English translation. I have been using draft translations from these volumes in teaching for the past fifteen years and hope to publish a larger collection of selected translations in the near future.

12. Some of these as yet unpublished manuscripts include various prayers and meditations; an early metaphysical work (1914) dealing with many of the same subjects as *Knowing the Spirit* entitled *Kashf al Haqā'iq* (*Unveiling of the Realities*); another study of the realities relating to each of the spiritual stages of religion, written in 1933, entitled *Haqīqat al-Asrār* (*The Reality of the Mysteries/Secrets*); and a detailed critical study of the foundational spiritual text (in Kurdish) of the Ahl-i Haqq Order, the *Kalām-i Saranjām*, based on Ostad Elahi's unparalleled manuscript collection. The centennial commemoration website (www.ostadelahi.com/English/Works) also mentions a collection of poems and a volume of interpretation of the Qur'an in Kurdish.

13. See the following revealing account from *Athār al-Haqq*, saying 1827 (chapter 23): "My father dictated the entire *Book of the Kings of Truth* [in 15,042 rhymed Persian couplets!] within a period of forty days. I still remember how he walked around the room, immediately and unhesitatingly reciting its verses while I very quickly wrote them down." Ostad Elahi's own corrected edition and commentary of that text (note 10) was based on his own, original handwritten copy of that poetic work.

14. Those extended question-and-answer sessions recorded in *Burhān al-Haqq* take up pages 245–655 of the full final edition of that work; the questioners are not identified by name, but often their nationality, profession, and the like are given to help contextualize their questions. The publications and videos prepared for the 1995 centennial commemorations include extensive firsthand accounts and impressions by Ostad Elahi's notable visitors during

this later period of his life, such as the musician Yehudi Menuhin, the choreographer Maurice Béjart, and so on.

15. *Burhān al-Haqq* continues to be studied today by ever-growing circles of readers, even outside Iran, who are primarily drawn by the universality of its underlying spiritual teachings, rather than the particular theological issues of its original context. That growing interest among wider, new audiences is an interesting commentary on Ostad Elahi's allusive remarks about the lasting importance of that work—as well as of *Knowing the Spirit*—in *Athār al-Haqq*, sayings 1894, 1997, and especially in the following saying:

> There are a great many secrets in (my book) *Ma'rifat al-Rūh* [*Knowing the Spirit*] that I haven't even mentioned to you my children, who are nearer to me than anyone. Only after I'm gone will people understand the real lasting value of *Ma'rifat al-Rūh*, *Burhān al-Haqq*, and the other books I've written. The more people's level of knowledge increases the more they'll discover in those writings. . . . Their importance will increase with each passing century. . . . I investigated each subject until I had completely mastered it and there was nothing left that I didn't know about it: that is my way of inquiry. [AH, 2076]

16. *Athār al-Haqq* itself provides hundreds of memorably anecdotal, often directly autobiographical illustrations of each of the major philosophical points developed in *Knowing the Spirit*. Indeed this procedure of communicating from the common ground of actual spiritual experience and lived example, rather than from the controversial ground of opinions and beliefs, is one of the most fundamental dimensions of all of Ostad Elahi's teaching.

17. Students of religion (i.e., of the phenomenological study of all religious traditions in all their dimensions, not just the very limited domain of official theologies) are well aware that this sensitivity is not at all dictated by the actual eschatological words and teachings of their prophets and scriptures per se and that within each religious tradition one normally finds, over long periods of time—especially within schools of actual spiritual teaching and practice—a vast spectrum of interpretations and understandings much more closely attuned to the actual observable range of human spiritual phenomena and experience.

18. Those directly familiar with Iranian popular culture, now and for centuries past, are well aware of the extraordinary extent to which people of all walks of life and educational backgrounds, today as in the past, are constantly discussing, as one of the most recurrent dimensions of *everyday* life, their own reflections on the deepest philosophical and spiritual issues, often supported by the taken-for-granted memorization of thousands of verses of profound metaphysical poetry (Rumi, Hafez, Attar, and so many others). During a recent taxi ride in Tehran—echoing the story that even the donkey-drivers of Florence once knew Dante's poetry by heart—I witnessed two housewives in the same taxi, returning from their evening shopping, heatedly

debating with a much younger religious scholar the true interpretation of Mulla Sadra's concept of "transsubstantial motion" (*haraka jawhariyya*: see chapter 3 of this translation), which is the philosophical foundation for many of the ideas elaborated here in *Knowing the Spirit*.

19. Because the vast majority of Ostad Elahi's originally intended Persian readers would have been educated within the Imami ("Twelver") Shiite religious tradition, the teachings he quotes here (as in *Burhān al-Haqq*) are normally drawn from the standard collections of sayings of the Imams of that tradition (see the first section of the bibliography in this volume). Readers familiar with the classical spiritual literatures of Sunni Islam (Sufi poetry, Ibn 'Arabi, etc.) will immediately recognize that there are immediate equivalents to almost all of the teachings cited here within the wider corpus of the hadith of the Prophet Muhammad. Those widely popular traditional sources from the vast body of Persian Sufi literature, which include the famous Persian spiritual poets, are more frequently quoted and alluded to throughout Ostad Elahi's (originally oral and private) teachings collected in the two volumes of *Athār al-Haqq*.

20. See the explanation and extended illustrations of this point in our extensive historical introduction (pp. 1–90) to *The Wisdom of the Throne: An Introduction to the Philosophy of Mulla Sadra* (Princeton: Princeton University Press, 1981; updated paperback edition forthcoming). Readers interested in a more detailed account of the various philosophical and spiritual traditions and conventions of esoteric writing that are assumed and drawn on throughout *Knowing the Spirit*, as well as additional background reading, should refer to that work and its bibliography. An equally representative, and slightly earlier, illustration of this same distinctive threefold approach, by the celebrated Persian poet, hagiographer, theologian, and interpreter of Ibn 'Arabi Jāmī (d. 898/1492), is also accessible in Nicholas Heer's translation, *The Precious Pearl: Al-Jāmī's "al-Durrah al-Fākhira"* (Albany, NY: State University of New York Press, 1974).

21. Informed readers should recognize the ways in which this apparent "commentary" format is the standard scholastic form for expressing one's *independent* ideas and thinking not only in classical Islamic cultures, but within the classical educated discourse of virtually every premodern literate civilization.

22. As already noted (note 18), it is difficult for Western audiences to appreciate the depth to which even—or should we say "especially"?—the nonliterate, popular culture of the Persianate Islamic cultural world, extending far beyond the boundaries of contemporary Iran, has long been profoundly shaped and impregnated by complex metaphysical traditions and religious concerns conveyed by locally pervasive forms of Sufism, poetry, devotional music, ritual, and practical spirituality. In addition to the marvelously telling illustrations of this cultural milieu provided throughout *Athār al-Haqq*, see especially Reinhold Loeffler's *Islam in Practice: Religious Beliefs in a Persian Village* (Albany, NY: State University of New York Press, 1988), the informed traveler's accounts—particularly relevant to the traditional cultural milieu of

Hajji Ni'mat and of Ostad Elahi's own formative years—richly provided by E. G. Browne, *A Year Amongst the Persians* (London: 1893), and J. A. Gobineau, *Les religions et les philosophies dans l'Asie centrale* (Paris: 1866). The relevant bibliography here could take up an entire book, but the essential point for understanding *Knowing the Spirit* is that Ostad Elahi was writing for a far wider audience, both seriously informed and profoundly concerned with the issues of his work and their treatment in the ambient philosophical and religious traditions, than we would now expect for a work of this type in contemporary Western cultures.

23. The traditionally accepted ways of speaking more openly of the phenomenological, experiential dimensions of the soul's journeys and process of perfection in Ostad Elahi's ambient culture were through the canon of Persian mystical poetry (figures such as Rumi, Attar, Hafiz) or else in direct, intimate exchanges between spiritual guides and their students (the subtle teaching process of *suhbat* recorded so vividly throughout *Athār al-Haqq*). Such potentially controversial matters were normally dealt with only by indirection and allusion in the formal written discourse (whether in classical Arabic or in the highly Arabicized Persian prose used here) of traditionally educated scholars. See the extended explanations and further illustrations of these assumptions and procedures of indirect communication throughout our study of an intimately related eschatological work of Mulla Sadra (note 20).

24. Ostad Elahi's primary emphasis on openly universal, philosophical (rational) arguments here in *Knowing the Spirit* is particularly evident in contrast with the more consistently theological discourse of his preceding published book, *Burhān al-Haqq*. One particularly vivid illustration of his distinctively spiritual application of this philosophical approach here is the way he actually evokes the classical philosophic proofs for the existence of God (in chapter 1 of *Knowing the Spirit*). It would be immediately evident to his original readers, who had memorized much more elaborate scholastic versions of all these arguments at the earliest stages of their traditional philosophical education, that Ostad Elahi's main interest here is not primarily "theological," since those standard arguments were long familiar to everyone, but rather to provoke his readers to a much deeper spiritual—and simultaneously intellectual—reflection on what *each* of those arguments leads us to perceive directly of the qualities and relations of God (or in traditional theological language, of the divine "Attributes" and "Names") that are immediately and universally visible in our experience of the natural and human worlds.

Thus arguments 1 through 3 for the existence of God in chapter 1 direct us to our wider human experience of the causal orders and regularities (i.e., the underlying laws) of all the realms of creation—including above all, in this context, our experience of the spiritual world; while argument 4—*not* normally included in the traditional theological and philosophical proofs of God at all—is unambiguously spiritual in its implicit references and intent. In particular, the novel way in which Ostad Elahi concludes his argument 5 (the familiar proof from intelligent cosmic design) is quite explicitly constructed here in such a way as to turn his readers directly to the intimate spiritual details of their own unique interactions with the divine (or in theological language, their existentially probative experiences of Providence and Grace) and hence to our uniquely human spiritual *responsibilities* for completing and fulfilling the divine purpose of the spirit's "Return." The individual results of that initial reflection in chapter 1 thereby set the stage for the wider eschatological conclusions to be drawn from that field of personal spiritual experience in each reader's reflections throughout the ensuing chapters 3 through 7.

25. See the historical references and illustrations cited at note 20 in this volume, especially for the fundamental role in the inspiration of Mulla Sadra's distinctive philosophical theses played by earlier Islamic spiritual figures, including the famous Sufi poets, spiritual teachers, and above all the central figure of Ibn 'Arabī, whose profoundly influential spiritual teachings mirror and anticipate the central ideas of Ostad Elahi in so many respects. Extensive illustrations of repeated thematic parallels to Ostad Elahi's spiritual teachings in the seminal work of Ibn 'Arabī, especially regarding the central practical role of spiritual intelligence and realization, are to be found in our recent volume *The Reflective Heart: Discovering Spiritual Intelligence in Ibn 'Arabī's Meccan Illuminations* (Louisville: Fons Vitae, 2005). Ostad Elahi's original learned readers would immediately recognize the recurrent references in *Knowing the Spirit* to the metaphysical thought of Mulla Sadra, both through the repeated employment of the distinctive technical vocabulary of Sadra's school (i.e., his explicit focus on both the "primacy of Being" and the "transubstantial motion" of all creation) and through the extensive supporting quotations and summaries drawn from more recent exponents of Sadra's school of thought, especially the famous Mullā Hādī Sabzavārī (d. 1878; see the bibliography in this volume).

26. It is important to keep in mind that most of the original readers of this particular work would *not* have had access to Ostad Elahi's own personal views and crucially relevant, lifelong personal experiences that have more recently been revealed in so much detail in the published volumes of *Athār al-Haqq*. Since, as already noted, the classical Islamic philosophers and theologians normally did not write *explicitly* of the full range of eschatological possibilities developed in chapter 7 here—and typically expressed a standard theological abhorrence of all the (often intentionally ill-defined) notions of *tanāsukh* ("transmigration": the subject of chapter 8 of *Knowing the Spirit*)—this book might well represent for more strictly intellectual readers, without personal experience of the relevant spiritual phenomena, their first serious encounter with an educated and persuasive articulation of those distinctive spiritual positions so boldly and carefully articulated throughout chapter 7.

27. As discussed later in this introduction, one of Ostad Elahi's most lasting lessons for modern readers as well may be his actual "process of investigation and verification" (*tahqīq*, in the language of this tradition)—or what we today might call "spiritual intelligence"—illustrated throughout *Knowing the Spirit* and his other works. In other words, he has carefully constructed this elaborate text not in order to convince all his readers to adopt this or that particular set of beliefs or concepts, but rather to start them thinking, observing

the relevant phenomena (spiritual, in this case), and then eventually testing and verifying the most fitting spiritual hypotheses and laws relating to those underlying experiences.

28. Indeed one quickly learns, in the process of teaching, that more explicit "explanation" often robs those allusions of any real spiritual or philosophic efficacy. It is like pointing out to a reader the clues in a mystery, or warning chess-players of their mistaken moves before they actually make them: little real learning can take place under those conditions.

29. That constant implicit cultural background of Sufi poetry is represented in this book by only two short lines quoted from Saadi and Hafiz. However, those two great Persian poets, along with the equally famous mystical teachers Rumi, Attar, and 'Abdullah Ansari (especially his famous *Munājāt*) are cited more extensively throughout *Athār al-Haqq*.

30. As we have stressed previously at note 22, it is essential to keep in mind that the popular familiarity of this vast corpus of spiritual poetry was until very recently inseparable from the even wider range of culturally and socially instituted forms of spiritual practice, guidance, and related ritual and devotional life once operative in many traditional Islamic societies, albeit widely destroyed in recent decades.

31. For example, this key, underlined statement near the end of chapter 3 in a way summarizes the argument of the entire work: *"the final point of the process of perfection of every creature is when it becomes the perfectly pure alloy, through integrating within itself the distinctive qualities of all the influences of the different natures of (all) the creatures, from the Source of the highest world on down to the bottom of the lowest world."* Yet Ostad Elahi nowhere explicitly points out to his readers all the absolutely essential connections between this brief remark and his longer metaphysical discussions of the "process of spiritual perfection" in chapter 7.

32. That is to say, the author does not explicitly point out that it is only through our concrete, necessarily particular and personal, spiritual awareness of the different "modalities" of spiritual growth and perfection detailed in chapter 7—and thus of the corresponding fundamental role of our recurrent human, earthly situations of testing and purification—that we can actually begin to comprehend how such central divine attributes as Justice, Wisdom, and Compassion (along with so many others) are in reality intimately related to what human beings actually *do* know and understand by those terms. This disputed topic of our human modes of awareness and understanding (or lack thereof) of the divine Names is, in the earlier Islamic philosophic, theological, and spiritual traditions familiar to Ostad Elahi's readers, one of the classic, recurrent illustrations of the distinctive methods of allusion and *tahqīq* ("spiritual investigation and verification") outlined previously at notes 24, 25, 27 and in the related books cited there.

33. See the historical background outlined in our study of Mulla Sadra in note 20 and the more detailed account of the inspiration and deeper motives underlying Avicenna's epochal, self-conscious "theologizing" of classical philosophy in "The Philosopher-Prophet in Avicenna's Political Philosophy,"

in *The Political Aspects of Islamic Philosophy*, ed. C. Butterworth (Cambridge: Harvard University Press, 1992), 142–188. Both Avicenna and Mulla Sadra (among many others) had major works literally entitled *al-Mabda' wa-l-Ma'ād* (*The Origination [of existence] and the Return [of the human spirit to God]*), and all their systematic writings follow the same basic order of exposition, from cosmology/ontology to eschatology/epistemology, which is faithfully mirrored in *Knowing the Spirit*. If much of the philosophical language and argumentation at the beginning of *Knowing the Spirit* seems vaguely familiar to some Western readers, that is because translations of Avicenna's works and interpretations of Aristotle formed an essential, lastingly influential element in the historical foundation of medieval Latin scholastic philosophy.

34. *Al-Hikmat al-'Arshiyya*: see the reference to our translation and contextual study of that work in note 20; the same points are developed at much greater length in each of Sadra's longer systematic works as well. Together with its companion summary of Mulla Sadra's ontological/cosmological ideas, the *Kitāb al-Mashā'ir*, this short work provided the most accessible and widely read introduction to Sadra's complex philosophical thought for educated Iranian readers throughout the past three centuries, as a common subject for both teaching and interpretive commentaries. Unlike Sadra's immense *Asfār*, its contents would have been immediately familiar to much of Ostad Elahi's traditionally educated original audience—as, indeed, it still is to some degree in Iran today, where we recently viewed a nationally televised popular game-show specifically devoted to questions about Mulla Sadra's works, biography, and philosophic theses; see also note 18.

35. See also the brief but pertinent remarks on Qur'an translation and eschatology in the note on the Persian text and translation conventions immediately following this introduction. For a representative cross-section of the many diverse later traditions of Islamic thought centered around this Qur'anic structure of the "Origination and Return" (see note 33), see the extensive selections included in the wide-ranging anthology of Sachiko Murata, *The Tao of Islam: A Sourcebook on Gender Relationships in Islamic Thought* (Albany, NY: State University of New York Press, 1992), or any of the numerous translations now available from the works of Ibn 'Arabi and his later interpreters. (See full details in our downloadable web-based volume *Ibn 'Arabī and His Interpreters: Historical Contexts and Contemporary Perspectives*, now directly available at www.ibnarabisociety.org/IbnArabi).

36. As, of course, are a great number of both the corresponding Sunni hadith and corresponding traditions of the Shiite Imams.

37. This is a point that Ostad Elahi develops at length throughout the more theological and scriptural discussions of his *Burhān al-Haqq*.

38. These spiritual phenomena are illustrated, of course, in profuse, often revealingly autobiographical detail throughout the oral teachings recorded in both volumes of *Athār al-Haqq*. Probably the best comprehensive introduction to the most lastingly influential theoretical accounts of that vast phenomenology of sainthood and spiritual guidance in later Islamic tradition are the ideas of Ibn 'Arabi carefully summarized in Michel Chodkiewicz's magisterial *The*

Seal of the Saints: Prophethood and Sainthood in the Doctrine of Ibn 'Arabī (Cambridge: Islamic Texts Society, 1993; originally Paris: Gallimard, 1986). At the concrete social and cultural level, the relevant literature available in English translation is now immense: for one starting point, see our "Situating Islamic 'Mysticism': Between Written Traditions and Popular Spirituality," in *Mystics of the Book: Themes, Topics and Typologies*, ed. R. Herrera (New York/Berlin: Peter Lang, 1993), 293–334.

39. The numerous international websites cited previously in note 4 that are now devoted to supporting the multifaceted constructive elaboration and application of Ostad Elahi's seminal ideas are one useful starting point, listing important creative efforts in many different areas of contemporary life. Equally noteworthy are the numerous volumes in an ongoing series (Foundations of Natural Spirituality) of books that his son, Dr. Bahram Elahi, has recently devoted to elaborating Ostad Elahi's spiritual insights using the more universal language of modern science and medicine. To date, that series includes *Foundations of Natural Spirituality: A Scientific Approach to the Nature of the Spiritual Self* (NY: Harper Collins, 1998); *Spirituality Is a Science* (NY: Cornwall Books, 1999); and *Medicine of the Soul* (NY: Cornwall Books, 2001). See also B. Elahi's general summary of Ostad Elahi's teachings in *The Path of Perfection* (revised edition, NY: Paraview, 2005).

40. See our discussion of Ostad Elahi's pioneering contributions in this area of spiritual ethics and religious understanding developed throughout *Orientations: Islamic Thought in a World Civilization* (London: Archetype, 2003) and more generally the contributions by internationally noted figures from many different related fields (music, psychology, literature, art, law, ethics, and religious studies) to the symposia held in Paris and New York on the occasion of the 1995 centenary celebrations, collected in the volume *Le Spirituel: pluralité et unité, actes du symposium* (Paris: Presses de l'Université-Sorbonne, 1996).

41. Philosophical readers will recognize the many correspondences here, and elsewhere, between Ostad Elahi's approach and that of Plato's dialogues.

42. Since there are now immense and rapidly growing literatures in each of these fields—not to mention the ongoing contributions of thousands of related practitioners in the many related medical and therapeutic disciplines—we may mention here only one particularly comprehensive and methodologically well-grounded work of this order, marked by its extraordinarily detailed correspondences with the observations of Ostad Elahi outlined in the last half of chapter 7 here (and greatly elaborated in the two volumes of *Athār al-Haqq*): Michael Newton's *Journey of Souls: Case Studies of Life Between Lives* (Minneapolis, MN: Llewellyn, 1994).

Notes to the Persian Text and Translation Conventions

1. This inclusion within a book of large excerpts of supporting textual material from other sources, which would normally be given simply as footnote references in modern, Western-style book production, is a standard feature of traditional Islamic scholarly writing—dramatically visible, for example,

throughout Mulla Sadra's monumental *Asfār* and similar comprehensive works—that was practically quite necessary in the age of manuscripts, before the modern world's recent easy access to books and electronic references.

2. For more details, see our study of "Qur'an Translation and the Challenge of Communication: Toward a 'Literal' (Study) Version of the Qur'an," *Journal of Qur'anic Studies*, 2:2 (2000), 53–68.

Notes to the Translation

Introduction

1. [The initial paragraphs here, following the traditional pattern of opening books with rhyming praises of God and then of the Prophets and saints, include many familiar Qur'anic phrases and divine Names (in Arabic) and their Persian equivalents. We have italicized here those sections that are directly quoted from the two Qur'anic suras (1 and 112) commonly recited in the daily canonical prayers. Translations of Qur'anic quotations throughout the rest of the book have been placed in italics and identified by the corresponding chapter (*sūra*) and verse (*āya*) numbers (e.g., 1:2 = *sūrat al-Fātiha*, second verse) in parentheses within the translation, unless a note is necessary for further explanation or contextualization of the quoted passage. Translations of the many other Arabic passages (proverbs, short prayers or invocations, philosophic principles, etc.) included throughout the text have simply been given within quotation marks (without italics), as with quotations and allusions in Persian. A single English translation has been given in the numerous passages where Ostad Elahi first quotes the original Arabic (of a Qur'anic verse, sayings of the Prophet or Imams, and so forth) and then gives his own Persian translation.]

2. *Burhān al-Haqq*, seventh edition, p. 185.

3. [Throughout this book, as in his other published works, Ostad Elahi has strongly stressed certain key ideas or principles, which are always given—both in the original Persian edition and in this English translation—in *italic boldface* (corresponding to his double-underlining in his original, handwritten manuscript). Those highlighted passages helpfully outline the essential structure of the author's own argument in this work. We should add that the terms translated as "religious" and "Religion" (*dīnī/Dīn*), here and throughout this book, refer specifically to the universal, intrinsic spiritual responsibilities of *all* human beings, and not to any particular set of historical traditions.]

4. (Quoted in Arabic from the book) *Kifāyat al-Muwahhidīn* [author: al-Quddūsī], vol. III, p. 52.

5. From the *Gulistān* (*The Rose-Garden*) of the famous Persian poet of Shiraz, Saadi (ca. 1200–1292).

6. *Mu'ād*: defined as "that which is returned (to God) on the Day of the Return." *Kifāyat al-Muwahhidīn*, vol. III, p. 83.

7. *Ma'ād*: defined as "the realm of (the spirit's) return and ultimate outcome or destiny" in *al-Munjid* and other Arabic dictionaries.

8. [*Āyāt*, the key Qur'anic expression used here, refers both to the "Signs" of God in all creation, and by extension to the individual verses of the Qur'an, as is further explained in Ostad Elahi's note here]: "Universal" and "particular" (*concepts*) refer to what only exists in the mind, not in external reality; while in external reality the "universal" includes its particulars, and the particular realities are among the particular manifestations of that universal.

Chapter 1. Establishing the Existence of the Divine Artisan

1. See the *Kitāb Falsafah-yi 'ālī* [by Javād Muslih, a Persian summary of the metaphysics section of Mulla Sadra's *Asfār*; Sadra's philosophy—which here largely follows familiar, long-standing Avicennan ontological arguments— underlies almost all the arguments summarized in this chapter], vol. I, chapters 6 and 7, 34–38; Mulla Sadra's *Asfār* (lithographed edition), vol. I, book 2, chapter 7, p. 34; *Asfār* (1960–65 printed edition), I, pp. 149 and following; Sabzavārī's *Sharh-i Manzūmah* (lithographed edition), pp. 60 and following.

2. [Ostad Elahi's reference in this second case is to those higher forms of purely formal and metaphysical "causality"—for example, the bringing into existence of the higher angelic Intelligences, and so on—that are not subject to the more familiar sorts of secondary causality operating in the material, temporal world.]

3. [*Māhīya*: literally, "*what* (a particular thing) is." In the technical philosophic language of Ibn Sīnā (Avicenna) and his later Islamic philosophical interpreters, which is employed throughout this opening chapter, all actually existent things are understood to consist of *both* "being" (*wujūd*) and a particular "quiddity" (sometimes translated as "essence"), which refers to "what" they essentially are.]

4. For detailed traditional philosophic proofs of the falsity of the notion of an endless circle of causes [the origin of the common English expression "a vicious circle"] or of an infinite chain of causes, see the appendix [in the Persian edition of *Ma'rifat ar-Rūh*], section 1, pp. 97–99.

5. [Here the author is referring to all the intrinsic distinctions of the divine attributes and qualities (the divine "Names") that exist eternally *within* the One unique divine Essence.]

6. [The explanatory subtitle of this and the following three arguments is taken from Ostad Elahi's own section headings in his original table of contents.]

7. The "intrinsic" character (of this universal natural order) is mentioned here because it is possible for the intrinsic, naturally determined order to be disturbed by accidental causes.

8. [That is, "caused" by a *higher*-order or ultimate cause (*'illa*), not by the complex of "intermediate" or proximate causes (*sabab*) on the same level of being; the following argument is only really clear and cogent if that fundamental distinction is kept in mind, particularly in regard to the ultimate form of causality actually in question here, which is that of "bringing into existence (from nonexistence)" or "giving being" (*ījād*).]

9. For the original Arabic of this saying, see the *Kifāyat al-Muwahhidīn*, vol. I, quoted in the Appendix, section 2, p. 99.

10. [Qur'an 2:99 and fifty-one other verses: the sheer number of the relevant Qur'anic passages concerning the divine "Signs" (*āyāt*) alluded to in Ali's speech quoted here suggests the repeated centrality of this type of cosmological-teleological argument in the Qur'an as a whole.]

11. [*al-dahriyyūn* and *al-tabī'iyyūn*: in the traditional terminology of Islamic philosophy, both of these expressions refer to those nontheistic thinkers who maintained that the recurrent orders of the natural, material world are in themselves self-subsistent and self-explanatory, without any need for an ultimate Cause or Creator.]

12. [The technical, philosophical language employed here assumes the larger Avicennan framework of the ontological proof outlined in the first argument. In that schema, the basic logical modes of "possible," "necessary," and "impossible," when applied to the ontological domain of existence or being, are shown to require an ultimate "preponderating factor" (*murajjih*)— the Necessary Being—to explain the obvious existentiating "preponderance" that has transformed each of the intrinsically "possible" or contingent beings into "necessary," actually existing ones.]

13. [Or "intentionally" (*ta'līmī*). As explained in the immediately following point 3, this latter distinction refers to phenomena that are the product of a consciously intentional plan and ordering process.]

14. [*Dalīl*, the technical philosophic term used to entitle each of these five sections, can simply mean a significant "sign" or "indicator"; that broader meaning is probably more appropriate to the range of spiritual experiences underlying this extremely allusive section.]

15. [*Hudūth* has the technical sense here of anything that "(newly) comes into being" at some point in time and that is therefore conditional upon time. The word translated throughout these arguments as "eternity" (*qidam*) refers more specifically to "*pre*-eternity," to what has already existed "*from* eternity," as well as without any limit in the future; the Qur'anic divine name of "the Eternal" (*Qadīm*), mentioned repeatedly in this section, likewise refers to that uniquely divine quality of *pre*-Eternity.]

16. Both examples are quoted (in the original Arabic) from the *Kitāb-i Shamsiyyah* [of Qazvīnī, the classic Arabic handbook of formal logic], p. 158.

17. For the original Arabic text of this saying, transmitted (by the famous Shiite hadith scholar Ibn Bābawayh) in *Tafsīr al-Burhān*, vol. I, see the appendix, section 3, p. 99.

18. [That is, direct descendant; a polite formula of respect for the Imam's lineage going back to the Prophet.]

19. See the appendix [to the original Persian edition], section 4, p. 101, for the full Arabic text of this saying (also transmitted by Ibn Bābawayh) from the *Tafsīr al-Burhān*, vol. II, p. 208.

20. [In the appendix (p. 102, note to section 4), Ostad Elahi cites the original Arabic of a great number of Qur'anic verses conveying this idea of

God's transcendence of all resemblance with the creatures, with only small changes in wording: 17:43; 6:100; 23:91, 37:159; 9:31; 10:18; 16:1; 30:40; 39:67; 28:68; and 52:43; 59:23.]

21. See the original Kurdish poem [and Ostad Elahi's Persian translation] in the Appendix, section 5, p. 103. [The translation of this poem reads as follows:

> We are (the symbolic Arabic letters) "Q" and "H."
>> We are traveling the path of "H" and "Q" (= *HaQQ*: Truth, God, ultimate Reality).
> We are always receiving the blessings of the Will of the (divine) King;
>> We are disciples of the Master of silk-weaving.
> The Master made a pact with me, on the weft of our covenant:
>> He looked at me with Beneficence, and handed me my weaving materials.
> His weaving is Loving-kindness and the path of faithfulness to that pact.
>> His Design is such that His action is without any injustice.
> If God helps and gives me good fortune,
>> I will take the weaving materials in hand and quickly finish weaving.]

22. [*Sayr-i takāmul*: Ostad Elahi introduces the meaning of this key expression in very general terms at the end of chapter 3, and it is then developed in much greater detail in chapter 7.]

23. [The philosophical principle originally quoted in Arabic here paraphrases several well-known Qur'anic passages of an eschatological nature.]

24. [Qur'an 7:172. Knowledge of this entire famous covenant-verse is presupposed here: *And when your Lord took* (all) *the descendants of the children of Adam from amongst them, and He made them bear witness against their own souls* (saying): *"Am I not your Lord?" They replied: "Yes indeed, we have sworn witness* (to that)*!" Lest you all should say on the Day of the Rising: "Surely we were heedless of this!"*]

Chapter 2. The Spirit

1. [*Nafs-i nātiqah*: "rational soul" is the standard Arabic translation for this classical philosophic term (as in Aristotle's *De Anima*), which was commonly used—but understood and applied in radically opposed ways—throughout the many very different traditions of later Islamic thought. As can be seen from the much wider range of meanings of "spirit" that follows, in this chapter and the rest of the book (as well as his other writings), Ostad Elahi follows a long tradition of earlier spiritual writers (whose most influential Islamic representative was Ibn 'Arabī) in *not* reducing in any way his consideration of the "Spirit" either to its visible human manifestations, or—even less—to the far narrower meanings of "soul" developed by Aristotle and usually assumed by most of his Avicennan interpreters. In this volume, precisely to avoid any possible misunderstanding, Ostad Elahi consistently employs the unambigu-

ous word *rūh* ("spirit") throughout, and only mentions the restricted human term *nafs* ("soul"), as he does here, when he is explicitly referring to and quoting the opinions of earlier Islamic philosophers (as is again the case in chapter 8).]

2. (The original Arabic of this definition is quoted here from the book) *Kifāyat al-Muwahhidīn*, vol. II, pp. 26 and 28.

3. [In the original Persian text, Ostad Elahi gives each of these following verses first in the original Arabic and then in his own Persian translation.]

4. [Each of the following sayings was also originally given in Ostad Elahi's original text both in Arabic and in his own Persian translation. Kulaynī's *Kitāb al-Kāfī* (*The Sufficient [Reference]*) is one of the most important and commonly cited classical collections of the hadith of the Imami Shiite Imams. It is divided into two major sections, *Usūl* (the "roots" or fundamental principles of the faith) and *Furū'* (the more specialized juridical "branches"). In the text of *Ma'rifat ar-Rūh* used for this translation, the complete, original Arabic text of each of the four following hadith from Kulaynī is quoted in full, along with its preceding chain of transmitters, in the appendix, sections 6–9, pp. 103–105.]

5. [Qur'an 2:125, 22:26, and 71:28. The reference to Abraham as *Khalīl Allāh* is at 4:125.]

6. [The original readers of this work would easily recognize and fill in the important allusions here to a key passage of the Qur'an (23:12–16, quoted further on at the beginning of the following section) that also makes the explicit and powerful connection to the larger subject of this chapter, the spirit's survival and ongoing existence after death:

Surely We have created the human being (insān) from an extract of Clay. Next, We made him a droplet in a secure resting place. Next, We made the droplet into a clot, then We created the clot as an embryo, then We created the clot as bones, then We covered over the bones with flesh. Next, We brought him forth in another creation—so blessed be God, the Most-Beautiful/Best of Creators! Next, after that, verily you all are dying. Next, on the Day of Resurrection, verily you all are being raised up!]

7. [The same Persian pronoun *man* must be translated into English as "I," "me," or "my," depending on its grammatical context.]

8. *Hawl al-muttala'*: (this Arabic expression) literally means "fear" and "the place of coming to see": in the technical language of the specialists in hadith, they use this term to refer to the (angels') taking of the soul at the time of death and the soul's being raised up to heaven. See *Kifāyat al-Muwahhidīn*, vol. III, pp. 38 and 40.

Chapter 3. The Gathering, Reawakening, and Returning (of the Spirit) in the Realm of Return

1. [As the author implies here, these specific words are not found directly, in these actual grammatical forms, in the Qur'an (except for *ma'ād*, which appears only once at 28:55), but were instead developed as technical vocabulary in later learned theological discussions of the related eschatological symbols in the Qur'an and hadith.]

2. ['*Ālam-i ākhirat*: this central, recurrent Qur'anic expression (*al-ākhira*, which appears 115 times) refers specifically to the "further" or "next" *life*, as contrasted with that dimension of earthly, bodily life that we ordinarily consider "lower" or "nearer" to us (*al-dunyā*, which also appears 115 times). Both adjectives describe, implicitly or explicitly, the same ongoing *spectrum* of life (*hayāt*), only viewed from very different perspectives. As a result, we should stress that the actual Qur'anic usage of these terms does not imply the sorts of radical temporal or spatial separation and opposition suggested by virtually all the usual English equivalents. In this translation, "this world" is ordinarily used for *dunyā* and "the other world"—or occasionally, "the spiritual world"—for *ākhirat*.]

3. [The standard philosophic term used here (*fā'il*) also means "maker," and in reality that meaning often conveys more concretely what is actually intended by this technical language.]

4. [This celebrated *hadīth qudsī*, or "divine saying," in which God speaks directly in the first person, is quoted here by Ostad Elahi in the original Arabic.]

5. [*Khalq* here means both "creation"—that is, the "object" of this knowing—and "the (human and other) creatures" who are the active, responsible "subjects" of this knowing.]

6. [The original readers of this work would immediately recognize essential Qur'anic references in the first two terms mentioned here, in addition to the final allusion (to 2:286), which the author goes on to elaborate explicitly. For the first term ('*usr*/anguish), see 2:185: *God wants you all to have ease-and-joy* (*yusr*), *not anguish*. For the second term (*haraj*), see especially (among a dozen verses on this theme) 6:5: *God does not want to place upon you all any* (unnecessary) *difficulty, but He wishes to purify you . . .* ; and 22:78: *He has picked you all out specially, and He has not placed upon you any* (unnecessary) *difficulty in Religion. . . .*]

7. [*Mabda'*: here this term can be taken either as referring directly to God or the Necessary Being from which all existents derive, or more broadly, to the larger "*process* of Origination" or divine Self-manifestation in all existence. In this second sense, the process of divine Manifestation corresponds to the complementary metaphysical "process of Return" (*ma'ād*), as the author goes on to explain in the immediately following section.]

8. [This separate section heading is taken verbatim from Ostad Elahi's own detailed table of contents. As explained in the translator's introduction, the technical philosophic vocabulary introduced in this section, which was readily familiar to the author's original readers, is drawn specifically from the well-known metaphysical philosophy of the "unicity of Being" elaborated by the interpreters of Ibn 'Arabī and especially the sixteenth-century Iranian philosopher Mulla Sadra as a systematic philosophical expression of the spiritual insights developed by many of the famous earlier Islamic mystics. In that perspective, all the beings of the world—and pre-eminently human beings— are seen as participating in the universal, progressive process of the "transformation of their substance" (*harakat-i jawharī*: literally "transsubstantiating change"). The processes and stages of the human spirit's evolution and spiri-

tual development first summarily outlined here are described in much greater detail in the long chapter 7.]

9. [Or "Existence" (*vujūd*). The emphatic quotation marks here are Ostad Elahi's own. Readers who may wonder at this point whether the "being" in question here is that of God or of some particular being (such as their own self) will notice in the course of the following explanations—including the more detailed elaborations in chapter 7—that the proper answer is almost certainly "both."]

10. It is "relatively" transcendent or immaterial (*mujarrad*), because the only *absolutely* transcendent, immaterial thing is God, and nothing else. Otherwise, all the other immaterial beings (*mujarradāt*) are "freed" (*mujarrad*) from matter and form, but not from other accidental qualities.

11. Here Ostad Elahi cites a list of fifty other Qur'anic verses on this subject of the (broader metaphysical) Return, in the appendix, section 11, p. 106 [2:28, 46, 156, 210, 245, 281; 3:83, 109; 6:36, 108; 8:44; 10:4, 23, 46, 56, 70; 11:4, 34; 19:40; 21:35, 93; 22:76; 23:60, 99, 115; 24:64; 28:39, 70, 88; 29:8, 17, 57; 30:11; 31:15, 22, 23; 32:11; 35:4; 36:22, 83; 39:7, 44; 40:77; 41:21, 50; 43:85; 45:15; 57:5; 89:28; 96:8.]

12. [Ostad Elahi's original audience would immediately recognize his allusion at this point to the famous Qur'anic account (at 7:172) of the primordial covenant all human spirits swore to God, before their earthly manifestation, which was constantly referred to (as *"last night"* or the *rūz-i alast*, the Day of *"Am I not your Lord?!"*) throughout centuries of earlier popular Sufi poetry and spiritual teaching.]

13. [As is more fully explained in the following paragraph, the reference here is to each creature's initial direct relationship to its Creator and to the way that existentiating process of creation and manifestation necessarily begins with a descending movement from the creature's original proximity to God. In the traditional philosophic and theological terminology employed here, these two cosmic movements of the spirit's original creative manifestation (*mabda'*) and subsequent return to God (*ma'ād*) are compared to two "arcs" or bow-shaped semicircles, which together form the "circle" of all existence. These same terms also allude directly to the famous symbolic expression *"two bow-lengths or closer"* (53:9), which is mentioned in the Qur'anic account of one of the Prophet's most important revelatory experiences.]

14. As already indicated in the preceding section, each creature's immateriality or degree of transcendence (*mujarrad*: literally, being "freed" from material form) is necessarily relative, since only the Creator can rightfully be called *absolutely* Immaterial and Transcendent.

15. [The traditional technical philosophical terminology here is meant to distinguish clearly between the more subtle, spiritual "prime matter" (*hayūlā ūlā*) necessary for all formal manifestation, even in the spiritual and imaginal realms, and the more familiar physical "matter" (*mādeh*) of this elemental world.]

16. [*Mulk* occurs some 48 times in the Qur'an, both in reference to earthly rulership granted—and taken away—by God (3:26, 38:20, etc.) and more frequently to *God's* ultimate "Kingship" or "Possession of the heavens and the earth" (2:107, 3:189, etc.). Based on those usages, this term came to be used almost

universally throughout the different schools of Islamic thought in reference to the lowest level of being, the sensible, material world or "this lower world" (al-dunyā).]

17. [Malakūt: see the Qur'an 6:75, 7:185 (both referring to the "Rulership of the heavens and the earth") and 23:88, 36:83 (both referring to God's having "in His Hand the Rulership of every thing"). In the cosmologies of most of the later schools of Islamic thought and spirituality, malakūt usually refers to the next level of spiritual, but still causal and formal, reality immediately above the sensible, physical world of mulk (see the previous note); this stage would therefore overlap with at least part of the spiritual "intermediate world" (barzakh) or "imaginal world" discussed at greater length in chapter 7. Since the actual intended meaning is not well conveyed by this literal equivalent, most English translators prefer terms such as "angelic," which better communicate the "intermediate" and spiritual dimensions of this realm of being. We have followed that practice (using "angelic") in those places where this term is used as an adjective later—primarily in quoting and explaining Imam Ali's reference to the human spirit (rūh) as the highest of four different souls: the "angelic soul," or nafs malakūtī.]

18. [Jabarūt (derived from the divine name al-Jabbār, at 59:23), lāhūt (derived from the all-encompassing divine name, Allāh), and hāhūt (derived from the common Qur'anic expression for the ultimate, ineffable divine Essence, Hū) are classical terms in all schools of later Islamic thought for the higher degrees or meta-causal dimensions of noetic and spiritual proximity to the divine Essence. See Ostad Elahi's own more directly "phenomenological" explanation of the realities underlying these terms given in the following note.]

19. [In his earlier book Burhān al-Haqq, pp. 140–141, Ostad Elahi describes these last four higher stages of spiritual realization (after the exoteric religious duties regarding life in this material world) as follows:

> The second stage is one in which praying is freed from verbal and bodily constraints, and penetrates the heart. Its result is a state of presence of the heart and spiritual illumination. It is more expansive and higher than the preceding stage. In other words, that is the (spiritual) world of the "angelic realm" (malakūt). . . .
>
> The third stage is one in which praying rises from the heart to the angelic Intellect, in which the being is freed from the constraints of matter and form. Then, in a purely immaterial state, it passes through the stage of the "Dominion" (jabarūt). . . .
>
> The fourth stage is one in which the being loses all awareness of itself and melts like a drop of water into the boundless Ocean of divine Unicity. There its soul becomes connected to the primordial Source of the truly Real. That is the stage of the truly Real (al-Haqq), and corresponds to the state of "God-ness" (lāhūt). . . .
>
> That stage ends up in the state of the (divine) "Essence" (hāhūt), which includes three other spiritual states before Perfection. It is only after having completed those states that one can

fully experience the eternal Grace, which is indescribable and unimaginable.

20. [The *dahriyyūn* and "naturalists" (*tabī'iyyūn*), already mentioned in chapter 1 are—in the technical terminology of Islamic philosophy—those avowedly atheistic thinkers who restrict reality entirely to the visible cycles and orders of the material, sensible world, the world of "endlessly repeating time" (*al-dahr*).]

21. Among those who are unsure (among the ancient philosophers) were the physician Galen and his followers.

Chapter 4. The Purely Bodily Return

1. [As explained in the appendix to the Persian edition (section 12, p. 112), the philosophers' objection of "the beast of prey and the person who is eaten" raises the extreme hypothetical case of just who (or what) will be resurrected (and either punished or rewarded)—for those theologians who defended a very literal resurrection of *exactly the same* bodily elements—if, for example, a beast of prey should eat a person of faith (or another animal who has recently eaten such a person).]

2. For a summary of the (Islamic philosophers') detailed objections concerning "the impossibility of bringing back what was annihilated," the self-evident impossibility of this belief, and others [and the theologians' standard replies to each of those earlier arguments], see the texts included in the appendix to the Persian edition, section 12, pp. 106–113.

[The standard, lengthy scholastic arguments brought together in this appendix—from *Kifāyat al-Muwahhidīn* and from the accounts of them included in Mulla Sadra's *Asfār*—were part of a centuries-old tradition of formal disputation between Muslim philosophers and theologians concerning the subject of the resurrection of the body, as that was understood by the theologians. Here is Ostad Elahi's concluding personal judgment (appendix, pp. 112–113) concerning those often clearly rhetorical arguments:

> Each one of the arguments brought forth by those who support the impossibility of bringing back what is nonexistent and those who would allow that merits further discussion and consideration in itself, since this topic (of the Return) is so difficult and profound that it cannot be so easily resolved. The only thing that could really bring about decisive certainty and remove any doubts, confusions, and uncertainty would be the immediately self-evident presence and actual reality of the Gathering, Reawakening, and Returning of all the creatures in the realm of the Return—in such a way that that reality would become subject to the unequivocal support of all the religious groups of the people of the Book. (Since that hasn't yet happened for these disputants in such an incontrovertible way), the (theoretical) possibility or impossibility

of bringing back what is nonexistent has no particular relevance
or influence on the subject we are now discussing.]

   3. [*Tīnat*: this clearly symbolic term mentioned in the following saying of Imam Ja'far could mean roughly the same as the Qur'anic "*Clay*" (*tīn*)
from which Adam was created, or—as the word normally does in Persian—
the "fundamental character" or "essential nature" of a thing, which may be
the intended sense here. At the beginning of chapter 5 (on the purely spiritual
Return), Ostad Elahi himself uses this same expression (*tīnat*) as a synonym
for the (immaterial) essential "self" of each creature, or the individual spirit
itself.]

   4. The original Arabic text of this tradition, with its full chain of transmission, is quoted in the appendix, section 13, p. 113. [See the discussion of Kulaynī's
classic compilation of sayings of the Shiite Imams, at chapter 2, note 4.]

   5. See the complete table of the above-mentioned 288 Qur'anic verses
(which theologians have usually taken to confirm the purely bodily Return) in
the appendix, section 13, p. 114, quoted there from Majlisī's immense compendium of Shiite traditions, the *Bihār al-Anwār* (*The Ocean of Lights*) ed. Amīn al-
Darb, chapter "On the Establishment of the Gathering," vol. III, pp. 187–190.

   6. Quoted (in the original Arabic) from Majlisī's *Bihār al-Anwār*, vol.
III, p. 202.

   7. Quoted (in the original Arabic) from *Bihār al-Anwār*, vol. III, p. 202.

   8. [The classical Qur'an commentators have given two possible read-
ings for the unusual Qur'anic expression here (*al-sūr*), referring either to the
archangel Isrāfīl blowing into his "*Horn*," or to God's again blowing into the
"*forms*" (of each person: *al-suwar*, which has the same Arabic orthography) to
restore them to life.]

Chapter 5. The Purely Spiritual Return

   1. [The *mashshā'ūn*, in the later traditions of eastern Islamic philosophy, actually refers to the highly influential school of later Islamic philosophers—whose most notable representative was Nasīr al-Dīn Tūsī—whose
system of thought is primarily based on the works of the renowned Ibn Sīnā
(Avicenna); Avicenna's famous argument for the existence of a "Necessary
Being" summarized in chapter 1 is one of the hallmarks of this highly influential school of Islamic philosophy. These Muslim philosophers were called
"Peripatetics"—in contrast to a range of more Platonic schools of metaphysical thought—because of Avicenna's primary reliance on the positions and
writings of Aristotle in the elaboration of his thought.]

   2. [*Masīr*: this key term referring to the ultimate *individual* destiny
of each human being occurs 28 times in the Qur'an, almost always in
eschatological contexts.]

   3. *Bihār al-Anwār* (ed. Amīn al-Darb), vol. III, p. 203; see the full Arabic
text quoted in the appendix of the Persian edition, section 15, p. 115. [Majlisī
only refers to the unnamed philosopher in that passage as "the commentator

on (al-Ghazālī's) *Maqāsid*" (*al-Falāsifa*: "The Goals of the Philosophers," an influential pedagogical summary of the philosophical system of Avicenna).]

4. [*Mujarrad*: transcendent or "freed" from the elemental matter of this world; see the notes to chapter 3 stressing the "relative" immateriality of all the spirits, in contrast with God's absolute transcendence.]

5. See chapter 2, part 3 above.

6. [*Nasha'āt-i ukhravī* in Persian, alluding to the original Qur'anic terms (29:20 and 53:47) quoted later in this same chapter. It is impossible to convey in a single English term the three equally important aspects of this key Qur'anic expression: it conveys, to begin with (especially in relation to God's creative action), the notions of "rising up, bringing forth, originating, growing, creating." But when applied, as it usually is in these chapters of *Knowing the Spirit*, to the specific characteristics of the vast dimension of imaginal/spiritual existence that constitutes the "other (spiritual) world," it refers simultaneously to the "objective" side of that realm—hence our translation as "*dimension(s)*"— and to the corresponding individual or subjective experiences of that realm, where we would instead tend to speak of "*perceptions*," or "*sensations*" or "*states*." All three aspects of this key term are further developed here and in related discussions in the following two chapters.]

7. (For this passage and the one immediately following), see *Kifāyat al-Muwahhidīn*, vol. III, p. 4.

8. [Or: "these general *spiritual sensations* are . . .": see notes 6 and 9 on the complex meanings of this key term here and throughout *Knowing the Spirit*.]

9. [*Nasha'āt-i khusūsī-yi ma'navī*: the substitution here of *ma'navī* for *rūhī* (both of which have been translated as "spiritual" here) further emphasizes the more specifically experiential, epistemological character of the phenomena discussed in this second section: *ma'nā* refers to the individual, specific spiritual "objects" of perception, whereas *rūh* (used in the immediately preceding section) stresses the perceiver and the general nature of the universal spiritual dimensions in question.]

10. Reference cited in *Kifāyat al-Muwahhidīn*, vol. III, p. 5.

11. *Bihār al-Anwār*, vol. III, p. 203. [Here it is important to explain that the "Majlisī" mentioned here (and earlier at notes 5 and 6 in chapter 4) was a famous and highly respected earlier Safavid theologian and learned compiler of Shiite traditions, who is normally viewed without any suspicion of bias toward the views of the philosophers in this or other religious matters. That well-known authority gives a special weight to the final sentence of his remark quoted here.]

Chapter 6. The Harmonization of a Bodily and Spiritual Return

1. [*Tahqīq*: depending on the context, this key term can include both intellectual "*verification*" and the more experiential spiritual forms of "*realization*," including their combination in the processes of spiritual intelligence. While Ostad Elahi does not explicitly name any particular thinkers or groups in this chapter, his original learned readers would immediately identify this

"combined" eschatological position and his unambiguously positive emphasis on *tahqīq* here with the familiar expositions of this position by Mulla Sadra (and his later interpreters), Ibn 'Arabi, and a wider range of earlier Sufi authors and traditions familiar to any reader of Persian.]

2. [The author here uses the Arabic proverbial expression "attacking (for show) in order to retreat."]

3. [The Persian text does not indicate explicitly where the summary restatement of this particular group's views ends, but the rhetoric suggests that it actually continues to the end of this short chapter.]

4. In chapter 2, part 3 above.

5. [As indicated at the first mention of these technical terms for the different levels of metaphysical reality at the end of chapter 3 (notes 16–19), the Qur'anic expression "Kingship" (*mulk*) usually refers to the world of the soul, while the world of divine "Dominion" (*jabarūt*) refers to the realm of the pure Intelligences and to the corresponding advanced stages of spiritual realization, which Ostad Elahi summarized in the important passage from *Burhān al-Haqq* already quoted in chapter 3 at note 19.]

6. [*Nāsūt*: this common term used in many schools of Islamic thought, on the same model as the names of the other metaphysical "levels" or dimensions of reality already mentioned at the end of chapter 3, refers to the lowest physical and material level of human reality, roughly corresponding to the world of the "Kingdom" (*mulk*) discussed at note 16 in chapter 3.]

7. [*Nafs-i ammāra*: the Qur'an (at 12:53) is the original source for this key expression in all later schools of Islamic spiritual psychology.]

8. [*Haqq*: all three English expressions are necessary here to convey the simultaneous and interrelated ontological, ethical, and metaphysical dimensions of this universal process of perfection.]

Chapter 7. The (Spirit's) Return by Way of the Process of Perfection

1. [The central Qur'anic expression used here, *al-Dīn*, refers consistently to the metaphysical origin and destiny, and corresponding responsibilities, of all creatures, not to what we normally call different historical "religions." *Dīn*, in that broad metaphysical sense, has normally been translated here as "Religion" (i.e., capitalized) at each occurrence.]

2. Such as the story of Abraham that is alluded to in the Qur'an, 2:259–260.

3. [See chapter 3 (at note 13) for an overview of the underlying conception here of the initial "descending arc" of creation or emanation (from the divine Source, *mabda'*) and the corresponding "ascending arc" of the spirit's Return (*ma'ād*).]

4. [The conceptions briefly alluded to here are explained in considerably more detail in the third modality—the process of perfection through gradual "accumulation"—presented later in this same chapter.]

5. Hafez, *Dīvān* (ed. Qazvīnī), number 486, p. 345.

6. From now on, whenever the "discerning spirit" is mentioned, we are referring to that spirit which is morally responsible for its good and bad actions.

7. [Here, as often in this book, Ostad Elahi first gives the original Arabic of the Qur'an, then his own Persian version and explanation. We have given only a single translation, but have included in the un-italicized parentheses within these translations the author's additional, very short explanations that are sometimes incorporated in his Persian paraphrase.]

8. [This description for this second major section of chapter 7 has been added here directly from Ostad Elahi's own detailed table of contents.]

9. [*Barzakh*: the meaning of this fundamental technical term, drawn from the Qur'an and earlier traditions of Islamic spirituality, is explained in some detail later in Ostad Elahi's description of this "first modality."]

10. The "delay" here refers to the fact that spirits that must leave their material body after a sudden death, suicide, insanity, and the like may remain for a certain period in a state of bewilderment and disorientation. In such cases there may be a delay before the transfer of that spirit to the intermediate world takes place.

11. In the technical terminology of the ancient Greek philosophers [according to the influential eschatological accounts of the "Illuminationist" Islamic philosopher Suhrawardi, whose *Ishrāqī* school also developed the technical expression *'ālam-i mithāl* or "world of immaterial images"], that imaginal world was called *Hūrqalyā*, referring to a (spiritual) realm other than the material, elemental world. See *Kifāyat al-Muwahhidīn*, vol. III, pp. 199–200.

12. [As explained in detail in the Fourth Modality, this Qur'anic expression (*God's is the all-encompassing Proof; al-hujjat al-bāligha*, at 6:129) is taken here to apply to the full span of *50,000 years* (Qur'an 70:4), which is allotted to each human spirit to complete its process of spiritual perfection.]

13. Just as it says in the Qur'an: *O those who have faith, be heedful of God and seek out the means to (reach) Him, and exert yourselves in His path so that you all might be saved!* (5:35).

14. This is like what is stated in the Qur'an: *He directs the divine Affair from heaven down to earth; then it ascends to Him in a Day whose extent is a thousand years of what you all count* (5:32). And also the following verse: *The angels and the Spirit ascend to Him in a Day whose extent is fifty thousand years* (70:4).

It is also transmitted in a tradition (going back to the Prophet) that someone asked the Messenger about this verse (70:4) mentioning this *"Day"* (of the Return) as long as *fifty thousand years*: "O Messenger of God, what a long day that is!?" The Messenger replied: *"By Him in whose Hand is my soul, that Day is made easy for the person of true faith. Indeed it is easier for the person of faith than one of the prescribed daily prayers in this world!"* [The full, original Arabic text is given in the appendix to the Persian edition, section 16, p. 115, with reference to six classical Qur'an commentary works in which it appears.]

15. [The words given in parentheses here are part of Ostad Elahi's own explanation in his Persian translation, given after the Arabic of the Qur'an in his original text.]

16. [*al-Sāfī fī Tafsīr al-Qur'ān*, by Mullā Muhsin Fayz al-Kāshānī, the famous Safavid poet, philosopher, and religious scholar, who was Mulla Sadra's disciple and son-in-law.]

17. See the full reference (including the original Arabic and the chain of transmission) in the appendix, section 17, p. 116. [Our translation here and in the following three paragraphs is based on the original Arabic texts placed in the appendix in the later Persian editions of *Ma'rifat ar-Rūh*.]

18. See the full references [which mention that the same saying of Ja'far al-Sādiq is also found in the *Tafsīr-i Sāfī* (by Muhsin Fayz Kāshānī: see note 16 in this chapter) and in the *Kifāyat al-Muwahhidīn*] for this and the following saying given in the appendix, sections 18 and 19, p. 116. [As indicated previously, Kulaynī's *Usūl al-Kāfī* is one of the standard compendiums of sayings of the Shiite Imams; the *Majma' al-Bahrayn* (*Meeting-place of the Two Seas*) mentioned immediately following (note 19) is another widely read collection of Shiite traditions.]

19. See the reference and Arabic text of this saying in the appendix, section 20, p. 116.

20. [See chapter 3 for the initial explanation of this universal process of the "transubstantial motion" (*harakat-i jawharī*) of all beings through the "arc of ascent" and Return to the Source that constitutes their path of gradual perfection (*sayr-i takāmul*).]

21. See the appendix, section 21, p. 117 for some (Kurdish) verses by Shaykh Amīr concerning the one-thousand-first stage (or "world") of the path of gradual perfection (*sayr-i takāmul*).

[In that appendix, in addition to quoting these short Kurdish verses, Ostad Elahi says: "For an explanation and commentary on those verses, see (our) book *Burhān al-Haqq*." The translation of that particular passage (from *Burhān al-Haqq*, seventh edition, p. 176) is as follows:

> *Forever the Reckoning of the thousand-and-one stages:*
>   *When the star of Sirius appears,*
> *One of those stages blazes up, and through that*
>   *a thousand sheets of "Bulgarian (leather)" become perfumed.*

The explanation of this (poem) is that "forever" means from the beginning of Creation to the Rising. The "Reckoning" refers to the thousand-and-one years (5:32) and the others alluded to in the Qur'an (at 70:4). "*Kū*" (in Kurdish) means "crossing" or "lane" or "neighborhood," but in the special language of these (sacred Kurdish poems) it always refers to the above-mentioned thousand and one spiritual stages. (In the popular belief of that time) the rising of "the star of Sirius" was known to have an extraordinary influence on certain times and places, including Bulgarian leather or parchment (the highest quality of leather). Thus the poet compares the transforming effusion of the divine Loving-mercy (*rahmat*) to the star of Sirius, and the thousand-and-one spiritual stages to (as many sheets of) "Bulgarian leather." The remaining imagery is clear from the context and needs no further explanation.]

22. The full reference in the original Arabic for this and the following saying of Imam Ali is given in the appendix, section 22, p. 117.

23. With the only difference that in this case he calls the last and highest of the four souls "divine and angelic" (*malakūtī*), rather than "divine and universal."

24. [See the sayings of Ali quoted at the two preceding notes.]

25. It should be explained that certain creatures are human-animals (*bashar*) physically, but because of certain specific causes, the fully human (*insānī*), angelic spirit is not breathed into their initial human-animal form. They live in a state that is intermediate between the human-animal and the fully human state, one that has been termed "body of clay, spirit of clay." As for when those specific causes are no longer operative, and what form that creature takes after they are removed, that accounting is simply in the hands of the "*nobly recording* (angels)" (82:11). With regard to this special state, in the *Shāhnāmah-yi Haqīqat* [*The Book of Kings of the Truth*], the late Hājj Ni'matullāh [Ostad Elahi's father] says, in verse 9092: "It has been ordained for those people from the start / body and soul both molded of clay."

26. See the full text of this saying given in chapter 2, part 2 above.

27. Although in the opinion of some people the spirit is breathed into the newborn only at the moment it emerges from the mother's womb, when it takes its first breath of air from the outer world.

28. Here the phrase "*in another creation*" refers to the moment when the spirit is breathed into and becomes united with the human-animal (*bashar*).

29. See the full Qur'anic text cited in the discussion in chapter 2, section 3 above.

30. As a group of philosophers and sages have said, since the angelic human spirit is different from the composite, contingent, natural bodily soul of the human-animal, the spirit always exists in the spiritual world *before* (its connection with) the contingent (bodily) soul—as is indicated by the Qur'anic saying: . . . Say: "The spirit is from the Command of my Lord!" (17:85). [Although Ostad Elahi does not more precisely identify the "philosophers and sages" in question here, the thesis of the pre-existence of the human spirits—that is, before their bodily, earthly existence—is a central theme in the philosophy of Mulla Sadra and Ibn 'Arabī, many earlier Shiite teachers, and above all, at a more popular level, throughout the familiar poetic writings and teachings of much of the wider Sufi tradition.]

31. [*Tanāsukh*: the various mistaken doctrines specifically included under this technical term of later Islamic thought are discussed and refuted in chapter 8. All of those theories have in common three assumptions: that this type of movement of souls takes place solely on Earth; that it can and does take place in "descending," or indeed even random, directions; and that it commonly involves the movement of human souls into lower forms of life.]

32. Some of the arguments showing the opposition between the doctrines of *tanāsukh* [all involving the purely earthly transmigration of human souls into lower forms of life] and the process of gradual spiritual perfection are briefly explained in the appendix (section 23, pp. 117–118), while a detailed exposition of the falsity of the belief in the transmigration of souls can be found in chapter 8 below. [All of the arguments cited here in the original appendix are actually reproduced at greater length within chapter 8.]

33. In other words, the (Qur'anic) expression *sijjīn* ("Prison") refers to the prison of Gehenna, while *'illīyīn* ("the Heights") refers to the most exalted

levels of the mansions of Paradise. [It is Ostad Elahi's Persian translation here that explicitly identifies this "Book" with the record of each spirit's *actions*.]

34. For a detailed explanation of these technical terms, see (Ostad Elahi's earlier book) *Burhān al-Haqq* (*Demonstration of the Truth*), seventh edition, pp. 172–178.

35. That is, the *actual* male and female correspond to men and women in the human species, or to male and female among the animals. "Metaphorical" types of male and female—like the sun and the moon, or grammatical and linguistic gender distinctions—do not concern us here.

36. [As indicated previously in point 6 and in the "Second Exception" discussed at the very end of this chapter, this phenomenon only happens in rare cases of special punishments.]

37. Shaykh 'Azīz al-Dīn Nasafī, d. 616 AH [1219 CE], cited on this point in the *Sharh-i Manzūmah* of Hajj Mullā Hādī Sabzawārī (lithograph edition), p. 314, and in *Riyād al-'Arifīn* [of Rizā Qulī Khān Hidāyat] (lithograph edition), p. 107.

38. For example, some members of the human species are born and raised in surroundings that do not allow them any sort of means of education and advancement and ease of life, while others are able to enjoy every sort of blessing from birth until the moment of their death. Likewise in the case of the different animal species, some of them are always predators while others are always their prey, some are strong and others weak, some are advanced while others are primitive, and so on. Those differences are always based upon the different (individual spiritual) "accounts" that have been alluded to in earlier discussions in this chapter.

39. [*Hujjat*: i.e., each human spirit's total period allotted for completing the process of spiritual perfection, as explained in points 1 through 9 of the fourth Modality section immediately above.]

Chapter 8. The Belief of the Proponents of Transmigration

1. [*Editor's note* (in Persian edition): What is mentioned in this chapter pertains to the basic principles of the ancient proponents of the transmigration of souls (*tanāsukh*). At the present time many new versions of this belief have come on the scene, each of which has attempted to conceal the weak points of this doctrine.]

2. Since some of the philosophers and sages use "soul" (*nafs*) and "spirit" (*rūh*) to refer to the same reality, whenever the word "soul" is used here instead of "spirit," or vice-versa, the reference is still to the same spirit (discussed in all the preceding chapters). [In fact, philosophers, following Aristotle—and including such famous philosophic proponents of transmigration as Suhrawardi—tended to use the term "soul" (*nafs*) to refer primarily to the living, "ensouled" powers of the material body. Since this chapter largely recounts the opinions of the proponents of *tanāsukh* (who usually carefully avoided the religiously charged term "spirit," *rūh*), this is the only chapter in which Ostad Elahi (citing those erring opinions) frequently refers to the "soul" (*nafs*). So it is important to keep in mind that those whose views are criticized

here would not necessarily have agreed with his identification of "spirit" with their understanding of the (embodied) "soul."]

3 [For the wider historical background of these expressions in Islamic thought, see *The Encyclopedia of Islam*, articles on *tanāsukh*, by Daniel Gimaret, and on *ma'ād*, by R. Arnaldez, as well as the famous philosophical work of Sabzavārī (English translation listed in our bibliography) cited at the next note.]

4. [Literally, "*The Versified* (summary of his philosophy)," a popular compendium of Islamic philosophy, with his own longer attached commentary (the *Sharh-i Manzūmah*, mentioned in several earlier references in this book), by this famous nineteenth-century Iranian thinker from the school of Mulla Sadra. The original verses are alliterative, rhyming, and therefore easy to memorize.]

5. [The particular attribution and description of the views specifically cited here, including the distinctive philosophic terminology, is in fact derived from the "Illuminationist" (*ishrāqī*), generally Neoplatonic writings of the medieval Iranian mystical philosopher Suhrawardi. Suhrawardi's eschatological conceptions—which he explicitly claims to derive from earlier traditions of ancient Iran and Mesopotamia—are very briefly summarized in the reference given in the appendix (section 24, p. 119) to the much longer discussions of this topic in Mulla Sadra's *Asfār*.]

6. [In Suhrawardi's distinctive philosophic terminology quoted here] "ruling light" means the transcendent, immaterial substance of the soul, and the "human castle" means the human body.

7. See the appendix, section 24, p. 119, for the summary of [Suhrawardi's] division of the states of human souls after their death, taken from the longer discussion of that topic in Mulla Sadra's *Asfār*.

8. [*al-dahriyyūn*: those ancient natural philosophers who would only acknowledge the endlessly repeated, visible cycles of earthly time (*al-dahr*) and material nature. See the earlier discussion of their views in chapter 1, the Third Argument.]

9. See the appendix, section 25, p. 119, for an additional list of the books of the philosophers refuting the notion of transmigration [primarily references from Mulla Sadra's *Asfār* and Sabzavārī's *Sharh-i Manzūmah*].

Bibliography

References Originally Cited by Ostad Elahi

By convention, all alphabetization ignores the Arabic article *al-*. Since Ostad Elahi usually mentions only the title of the sources he cites (rather than the author), and since many of his references are to older Iranian lithographed editions no longer accessible even in most university libraries, I have added cross-references listing his sources *by the title he actually employs*, as well as by author. The older lithographed texts commonly used by Iranian scholars until very recently often did not have details about a specific publisher, place, or sometimes even a date of publication. In a few cases where the older lithographed copies he cites were not available, we have had to mention more recent printed editions. In addition, when an English translation of a work he cited is now available (as for Sabzavārī), that translation has also been mentioned after the original text for readers who may wish to explore further some of the philosophical background to this work. Hejira dates, unless otherwise specified, are the normal lunar ones, while *solar* Hejira dates, commonly used for modern Iranian publications, are designated by the abbreviation AHS; all Hejira dates are followed by the their Common Era equivalents. Finally, as explained in the initial note on the Persian text and translation conventions at the end of our introduction, we have followed a simplified version of the standard scholarly transliteration system (*IJMES*/Library of Congress) for Arabic titles and premodern authors' names (i.e., eliminating those transliteration characters requiring a dot under certain consonants).

Asfār [see Sadra, Mulla.]
al-Bahrānī, Hāshim b. Sulaymān. *al-Burhān fī Tafsīr al-Qur'ān*. Tehran (3 volumes): n.d.
Bihār al-Anwār [see Majlisī.]
al-Burhān fī Tafsīr al-Qur'ān [see al-Bahrānī.]
Burhān al-Haqq [see Elahi.]

Elahi, Ostad [= Nūr 'Alī Elāhī]. *Āthār al-Haqq* (*Traces/Influences of the Truth*), ed. Bahram Elahi. Tehran: Tāhūrī, 1357 AHS/1978 (vol. 1); Tehran: Jayhūn, 1991 (vol. 2).

———. *Burhān al-Haqq* (*The Demonstration of the Truth*). 1st ed. Tehran: Tāhūrī, 1342 AHS/1963; 7th ed. Tehran: Jayhūn, 1366 AHS/1987.

———. *Ma'rifat ar-Rūh* (*Knowing the Spirit*). 1st ed. Tehran: Tāhūrī, 1969; 3rd ed. [used for this translation], Tehran: Jayhūn, 1371 AHS/1992.

Falsafah-yi 'ālī [see Muslih.]

Gulistān [see Saadi.]

Hafez [= Shams al-Dīn Muhammad Hāfiz-i Shīrāzī]. *Dīvān*, ed. Qazvīnī and Qāsim-ghanī. Tehran: Zuvvār, n.d.

Hidāyat, Rizā Qulī Khān. *Riyād al-'Ārifin*. Tehran: 1334 AHS/1955.

Jayhūnābādī, Hajj Ni'matullāh. *Shāhnāmah-yi Haqīqat* (*The Book of Kings of the Truth*). Tehran: Husseini, 1346 AHS/1967 [together with Ostad Elahi's commentary, *Haqq al-Haqā'iq*: see the following list of works cited in the translator's introduction and notes].

al-Kāfi [see Kulaynī.]

al-Kāshānī, Mullā Muhsin Fayz. *al-Sāfī fī Tafsīr al-Qur'ān*. Lithograph ed. Tehran: 1226/1847.

Kifāyat al-Muwahhidīn [see al-Quddūsī.]

Kulayni, M. b. Ya'qūb. *al-Usūl min al-Kāfī* [the "fundamental principles" section from *The Sufficient* (collection of Shiite hadith)], ed. Mustafavī (4 volumes). Tehran: n.d.

al-Majlisī, Muhammad Bāqir. *Bihār al-Anwār* (*The Ocean of Lights*). Tehran: Amīn al-Darb, 1305–1315/1887–1898.

Manzūmah [see Sabzavārī.]

Muslih, Javād. *Kitāb-i Falsafa-yi 'ālī, yā Hikmat-i Sadr al-Muta'allihīn* [*The Transcendent Philosophy*, a Persian summary of Mulla Sadra's *Asfār*]. Tehran: 1331 AHS/1952.

Qazwīnī, Najm al-Dīn Dabīrān Kātibī. *al-Shamsiyya fī-l-Mantiq* [the classical Arabic handbook of formal logic]. Lithograph ed. Istanbul: 1312/1933.

al-Quddūsī, Ismā'īl b. A. al-'Alawī. *Kifāyat al-Muwahhidīn fī 'Aqā'id al-Dīn* [in Persian]. Tehran (3 volumes): 1332 AHS/1953.

Riyād al-'Ārifin (*The Garden of the Mystics*) [see Hidāyat.]

Saadi. *Gulistān* (*The Rose-Garden*).

Sabzavārī, Mullā Hādī. *Sharh-i Manzūmah* [= *Sharh Ghurar al-Farā'id*] (*The Commentary on the "Versified"* [Summary of Philosophy]), eds. T. Izutsu and M. Mohaghegh. Tehran: McGill University Tehran Branch, 1348 AHS/1969.

———. *The Metaphysics of Sabzavārī*, translation of above by T. Izutsu and M. Mohaghegh. Delmar, NY: Caravan Books, 1977.

Sadra, Mulla [= Sadr al-Dīn Muhammad al-Shīrāzī]. *Kitāb al-Asfār al-Arba'a al-'Aqliyya fī al-Hikma al-Muta'āliyya*, (*The Book of the Four Intellective Journeys Through the Transcendental Wisdom*), ed. R. Lutfi (9 volumes). Qum: 1378–1389/1958–1969.

Shāhnāmah-yi Haqīqat [see Jayhūnābādī.]

Shamsiyya [see Qazvīnī.]
Sharh-i Manzūmah [see Sabzavārī.]
Tafsīr al-Burhān [see al-Bahrānī.]
Usūl al-Kāfī [see Kulaynī.]

Works Cited in the Translator's Introduction and Notes

When possible, reference has been given here and in the introduction itself primarily to sources and translations now available in English; however, several of the books cited here are now also available in French and other languages.

Browne, Edward G. *A Year Amongst the Persians*. London, 1893.
Chodkiewicz, Michel, tr. L. Sherrard. *Seal of the Saints: Prophethood and Saint-hood in the Doctrine of Ibn 'Arabī*. Cambridge: The Islamic Texts Society, 1993.
During, Jean. *L'âme des sons: L'art unique d'Ostad Elāhī (1895–1974)*. Gordes: Editions le Relié, 2001.
Elahi, Bahram. *Foundations of Natural Spirituality: A Scientific Approach to the Nature of the Spiritual Self*. NY: Harper Collins, 1998.
———. *Medicine of the Soul: Foundations of Natural Spirituality* [III]. NY: Cornwall Books, 2001.
———. *The Path of Perfection*. NY: Paraview, 2005.
———. *Spirituality Is a Science: Foundations of Natural Spirituality* [II]. NY: Cornwall Books, 1999.
———. *The Way of Light: The Path of Nur Ali Elahi*. Shaftesbury: Element, 1993.
Elahi, Ostad (Nūr 'Alī Elāhī). *Athār al-Haqq (Traces/Influences of the Truth)*, ed. B. Elahi. Tehran: Tāhūrī, 1357 AHS/1978 (vol. 1); Tehran: Jayhūn, 1370 AHS/1991 (vol. 2).
———. *Burhān al-Haqq (The Demonstration of the Truth)*. 1st edition, Tehran: Tāhūrī, 1342 AHS/1963; 7th ed., Tehran: Jayhūn, 1366 AHS/1987.
———, tr. C. Deville. *Connaissance de l'âme*. Paris: L'Harmattan, 2001.
———. *Haqq al-Haqā'iq, yā Shāhnāmah-yi Haqīqat* (commentary on and edition of *Shāhnāmah-yi Haqīqat*). Tehran: Husseini, 1346 AHS/1967.
———. *Ma'rifat ar-Rūh (Knowing the Spirit)*. 1st edition. Tehran: Tāhūrī, 1969; 3rd ed. [used for this translation], Tehran: Jayhūn, 1371 AHS/1992.
———. *100 Maxims of Guidance* (selections from *Āthār al-Haqq*). Paris: Robert Laffont, 1995.
———. *Words of Faith: Prayers of Ostad Elahi* (selections from *Āthār al-Haqq*). Paris: Robert Laffont, 1995.
Encyclopedia of Islam. CD-ROM ed., Leiden: Brill, 2001.
Gobineau, Comte J. A. *Les religions et les philosophies dans l'Asie centrale*. Paris: 1866.
al-Jāmī, 'Abdurrahmān, tr. N. Heer. *The Precious Pearl: Al-Jāmī's al-Durrah al-Fākhirah*. Albany, NY: State University of New York Press, 1979.
Jayhūnābādī, Hajj Ni'matullāh. *Shāhnāmah-yi Haqīqat (The Book of Kings of the Truth)*. Tehran: 1346/1967 [published together with Ostad Elahi's commentary, *Haqq al-Haqā'iq*].

Loeffler, Reinhold. *Islam in Practice: Religious Beliefs in a Persian Village*. Albany, NY: State University of New York Press, 1988.

Morris, James W. "L'éveil de l'intelligence spirituelle et les dimensions du processus éthique selon Ostad Elahi." In *Dieu a-t-il sa place dans l'éthique?*, ed. E. During, 86–99. Paris: L'Harmattan, 2002.

———. "La Pensée d'Ostād Elahi." In *Le Spirituel: pluralité et unité, actes du symposium* (Cahiers d'Anthropologie Religieuse, ed. M. Meslin, volume 5), 137–147. Paris: Presses de l'Université, 1996.

———. *The Reflective Heart: Discovering Spiritual Intelligence in Ibn 'Arabī's Meccan Illuminations*. Louisville: Fons Vitae, 2005.

———. *Orientations: Islamic Thought in a World Civilisation*. London: Archetype, 2004.

———. "The Philosopher-Prophet in Avicenna's Political Philosophy." In *The Political Aspects of Islamic Philosophy*, ed. C. Butterworth, 142–188. Cambridge: Harvard University Press, 1992.

———. "Situating Islamic 'Mysticism': Between Written Traditions and Popular Spirituality." In *Mystics of the Book: Themes, Topics and Typologies*, ed. R. Herrera, 293–334. New York/Berlin: P. Lang, 1993.

———. "Qur'an Translation and the Challenge of Communication: Toward a 'Literal' (Study) Version of the Qur'an." In *Journal of Qur'anic Studies*, 2:2 (2000), 53–68.

———. *The Wisdom of the Throne: An Introduction to the Philosophy of Mulla Sadra*. Princeton: Princeton University Press, 1981.

Murata, Sachiko. *The Tao of Islam: A Sourcebook in Gender Relations in Islam*. Albany, NY: State University of New York Press, 1992.

Newton, Michael. *Journey of Souls: Case Studies of Life Between Lives*. Minneapolis: Llewellyn, 1994.

Sadra, Mulla [= Sadr al-Dīn Muhammad al-Shīrāzī]. *Kitāb al-Asfār al-Arba'a al-'Aqliyya fī al-Hikmat al-Muta'āliyya* (*The Book of the Four Intellective Journeys Through the Transcendental Wisdom*). Ed. R. Lutfī (9 volumes). Qum, 1378–1389/1958–1969.

———. *The Metaphysics of Mulla Sadra*, translation [of *K. al-Mashā'ir*] by P. Morewedge. Binghamton, NY: Institute of Global Cultural Studies, 1992.

———, tr. James W. Morris. *The Wisdom of the Throne: An Introduction to the Philosophy of Mulla Sadra*, Princeton: Princeton University Press, 1981. [Includes translation of *al-Hikmat al-'Arshiyya*.]

Sabzavārī, Mullā Hādī. *The Metaphysics of Sabzavārī*, translation [of *Sharh-i Manzūmah*] by T. Izutsu and M. Mohaghegh. Delmar, NY: Caravan Books, 1977.

Unicity [1995 Ostad Elahi centennial commemoration volume]. Paris: Robert Laffont, 1995.

www.fondationostadelahi.org
www.ibnarabisociety.org/IbnArabi
www.nourfoundation.com;
www.ostadelahi.com
www.saintjani.org.

Index